Praise for
Rattled

"Trish Berg's advice will turn you from rattled to relaxed. Her solid tips and sense of humor make Rattled the perfect book for new moms."

—TIM BETE, author of *In the Beginning…There Were No Diapers* and *Guide to Pirate Parenting*

"Honest, informative, humorous, well-researched, encouraging, and practical are some of the words that describe *Rattled*. We can never have enough high-quality childrearing books and Trish Berg has outdone herself in this modern manual on capable, competent parenting in the first year. I recommend it."

—BRENDA NIXON, speaker and author of *Parenting Power in the Early Years*

"This precious book comes straight from the heart. It's personal stories, humor, and excellent tips and insights kept me reading…and smiling…nodding in agreement. Thank you, Trish, for this most wonderful gift to first year mothers."

—MICHELE STEINHAUSER, author and founder of Club M.A.W.–Encouraging, Equipping and Connecting Mothers and Wives

"Baby's first year is amazing, thrilling, sweet, and completely discombobulating! With Trisha Berg's help, though, new and new-again mommies can navigate the ups and downs of their [...] with savvy, a sense of humor, and spiritual gr[...]

—LORILEE CRAKER, author of nine [...] *We Should Do This More Often* an[...] *Minivan: Revving Up Your Marri[...]*

"*Rattled* is the perfect resource for an overwhelmed new mom. Trish Berg has broken down helpful information into bite-sized portions—perfect for a mom who desperately needs encouragement and practical help but only has moments of time to read. Trish has provided something for everyone—practical tips, humorous stories, and advice from a mom who's been there."

—GLYNNIS WHITWER, senior editor Proverbs 31 Ministries, author of *work@home: A Practical Guide for Women Who Want to Work from Home*

"Trish Berg has crafted the perfect mommy manual—engaging, informative, encouraging and best of all, without a hint of intimidation or guilt-producing rhetoric! All first-time mommies in my circle of friends will receive this gem as a gift as soon as they return home from the hospital or adoption agency!"

—KAREN EHMAN, national speaker for Proverbs 31 Ministries and Hearts at Home, author of *A Life That Says Welcome* and *The Complete Guide to Getting and Staying Organized*

"Kind, sweet, and funny—these words describe both this book and its author. Trish Berg knows first-hand both the fun and frustrations of motherhood, and her heart of encouragement shines through these pages. *Rattled* offers new moms some wise advice tempered with refreshing honesty, and reminds moms to keep their sense of humor while offering practical ways to connect with the God who loves them."

—KERI WYATT KENT, author of *Breathe: Creating Space for God in a Hectic Life,* and *God's Whisper in a Mother's Chaos*

RATTLED

Surviving Your Baby's First Year
Without Loosing Your Cool

TRISH BERG

MULTNOMAH
BOOKS

RATTLED
PUBLISHED BY MULTNOMAH BOOKS
12265 Oracle Boulevard, Suite 200
Colorado Springs, Colorado 80921
A division of Random House Inc.

Scripture quotations are taken from the Holy Bible, New International Version®. NIV®.
Copyright © 1973, 1978, 1984 by International Bible Society. Used by permission of
Zondervan Publishing House. All rights reserved.

ISBN 978-1-59052-913-3

Copyright © 2008 by Trish Berg

MULTNOMAH is a trademark of Multnomah Books and is registered in the U.S. Patent and
Trademark Office. The colophon is a trademark of Multnomah Books.

Library of Congress Cataloging-in-Publication Data
Berg, Trish.
    Rattled / Trish Berg.
        p. cm.
    Includes bibliographical references and index.
    ISBN: 978-1-59052-913-3 (alk. paper)
    1. Mothers—Religious life. 2. Motherhood—Religious aspects—Christianity.
I. Title.
    BV4529.18.B46 2008
    248.8'431—dc22

                                            2007030154

Printed in the United States of America
2008—First Edition

10 9 8 7 6 5 4 3 2 1

To Mike
Thanks for giving me your heart
wrapped up in the four sweetest packages
I could imagine—our children. 1 Corinthians 13:13

CONTENTS

ADDITIONAL RESOURCES

ACKNOWLEDGMENTS

A book is born from the hopes, dreams, and commitment of many. This project would never have evolved without the vision, energy, and passion from the team at Multnomah. I'm forever thankful to Brian Thomasson, Kimberly Brock, Thomas Womack, Lisa Bowden, Natalie Johnson, and everyone at Multnomah who partnered with me to help moms find the joy in their journey. And special thanks to my editor, Steffany Woolsey, for making my words sing.

To my agent, Les Stobbe, for guiding my career, opening doors for my writing, and following God's will at every turn.

To my husband, Michael, for encouraging me, always leading me closer to Christ, and becoming Mr. Mom for a while, so I could write a book on motherhood.

To my children—my biggest prayer is that I'm the mom you need me to be. Hannah, I cherish your compassion, your honesty, and your tender heart. Sydney, I adore your inner beauty, creativity, and love for life. Colin, I'm awed by your neverending joy, your heart for people, your loving spirit. Riley, I love watching you jump into life headfirst, and I can't wait to see the beautiful little girl inside your heart blossom.

To my parents, Mom and Dad Pearson—thank you for loving me through a lifetime of changes and teaching me to reach for the stars. To Mom and Dad Berg—thank you for raising your son to be a man of God and for loving me as your daughter. To my sister, Liz—thank you for always being by my side through life's ups and downs. To my sisters-in-law, Lisa, Jen, and Mary Beth—thanks for loving our family and bringing joy into our lives. And to Great-grandma Brillhart—thank you for teaching me what it means to faithfully live life to its fullest.

To my girlfriends, who bless my life with their faith, friendship, and encouragement—Teri, Carla, Nann, Kelly, Amy, Barb, Gail, Diane, Lisa, Erin, Megan, Nancy, Jen, and all the MOPS moms I have been blessed to meet (especially the women of Northview CMA MOPS). To MOPS International, especially Elisa Morgan and Beth Lagerborg—for opening so many doors for my writing and speaking. To my Camp Luther family and the congregation of St. Michael's Lutheran Church—thank you for living out your faith in my life.

To my column editors, Lance White and Lydia Gehring, and to all my column fans in Ohio, thank you for allowing me to share my life with you each week. To my writer friends—Karen Robbins, Cathy Messecar, Leslie Wilson, Brenda Nixon, Terra Hangen, Lori Scott, Heather Ivester, Tim Bete, Mary DeMuth, Beth Jusino, and Keri Wyatt Kent—thank you for mentoring, encouraging, and praying for me.

Thanks to my crack editing team and to all the moms who shared their stories with me for *Rattled*. Your words will touch the hearts of moms everywhere.

Most of all, to my Lord and Savior, Jesus Christ, who has blessed me beyond my wildest dreams. I pray my words are Your words, and that they touch families everywhere.

—Trish Berg

Welcome to the Wild Side

The wild side of life. A place where sleep is elusive, adventure lies around every corner, and your nights are suddenly filled with endless parties and soirees. (That is, parties for two featuring milk and lullabies.)

Welcome to motherhood, a lifelong adventure that many enter into but few are truly prepared for: an exhausting, overwhelming escapade in diaper changing and snotty-nose wiping. A breast-feeding, bottle-feeding, twenty-four-hours-a-day on-demand job that will drain every ounce of energy you have—and then some. (Sounds glamorous, doesn't it?)

So why do we take the plunge? Why do so many of us enter willingly into this alternate reality?

Plain and simple: love.

When you give birth to or adopt your new baby, it's as if you've given legs to your heart. And now your heart is out there in the great big world and must be cared for, protected, and loved. What do you get in return? A precious little baby who looks up at you with the most unadulterated adoration imaginable. You are his universe, and suddenly he is yours too.

On this journey to the wild side, all new moms can count on one thing: newborns are exhausting. They cry a lot (especially at three a.m.), they spit up milk on your shoulder, and their diapers will inevitably leak all over your pants during the Sunday morning sermon. But then there are those moments when that stinky little spit-up machine lies perfectly still across your chest, arms draped over your sides, and drifts off to sleep. Ah, love.

But babies grow up. New moms will soon face crayon marks on the walls, toys flushed down the toilet, muddy footprints tracked through the kitchen, and crumbs under every couch cushion. However, before you can move on to the chaos and clutter of the toddler years, you must survive the first year of motherhood—ideally without losing your cool. Life is too short not to enjoy what you have today, and motherhood too fleeting to get mired in frustration. Blink once, and your baby is a toddler. Blink twice, and she's in college.

This book is about simplifying, learning from mistakes, and becoming the mom God wants each of us to be. I want to help you not only survive your first year of motherhood but to delight in being a mom the way God intended. In *Rattled,* I offer information and advice from moms who have been there, answers to your questions from doctors and experts, and resources for further study. I also hope you can find humor in the small struggles we all inevitably face.

I know that you are busy and your time is precious. With that in mind, I've designed each chapter to resemble what I call a "Motherhood Survival Kit" (boy, did I need one of these with my firstborn!). If you were to be thrown out into the wilderness, the four basic things you would need to survive are water, food, fire, and shelter. Well, you've been thrown into the wilderness of motherhood, and to survive your baby's first year you will need:

- *Water from the Word.* Bible verses at the beginning of each chapter remind you to focus on God's Word through the mommy adventures that lie ahead.
- *Food for Thought.* Facts and statistics about the first year of motherhood will intrigue and inspire you.
- *Faith on Fire.* A closing prayer at the end of every chapter reminds you to lean on Jesus throughout your journey.

- *Shelter from the Storm.* Stories and advice from moms across the country will make you laugh, cry, and remember you're not alone on this mothering journey.
- *First-Aid Kit.* These practical tips will help you simplify life as a mom—kind of like mom-size Band-Aids.
- *SOS (Spiritual Opportunity to Savor).* In the wilderness you send out an SOS for help. We need to ask God for help too—so at the end of every chapter I've added a mom-sized devotional, a Spiritual Opportunity to Savor. This will offer busy moms like you the opportunity to renew and refresh your spiritual life.

Added Bonus

But wait, there's more! At the end of *Rattled,* you will find several resource sections loaded with tons of information on:

- *Miscarriage.* Recounts my own heartbreaking story and how I found hope in my despair through God's love.
- *Your Baby's Development.* Details your baby's development for each month during his first twelve months.
- *Your Compass.* Contains all the resources you'll need to survive the first year with your baby.

Welcome to the wild side of life called motherhood, loaded with dirty diapers, stinky spit up, and rarely enough slumber. You will be stressed and stretched further than you ever imagined. Some days you will wonder if you have what it takes to be a mom. Rest assured you do! So enjoy the most amazing love this side of heaven, wrapped up in the tiniest, sweetest little package called a baby!

STOP

Before you read any further, take this quick test to see what stage of motherhood you are in. Check all that apply to you and then add up your total check marks at the end.

0–1 Points

You are probably not a mom yet. However, you may be newly pregnant or have nieces and nephews putting you through mommy boot camp. If you're starting to freak out about the whole motherhood thing, let me assure you that watching shows on PBS Kids (and even enjoying it) isn't such a stretch.

Mom Test 101

☐ Bedtime stories and goodnight prayers last longer than an opera.

☐ You haven't slept through the night in months, and you can't remember the last time you curled your hair or put on makeup.

☐ You are awakened each morning by someone standing two inches from your nose, breathing on you, scaring you half to death.

☐ You can change a diaper faster than a rodeo cowboy can rope a calf.

☐ You have stretch marks in places you didn't know could stretch.

☐ You're still holding on to your before-kids jeans with the hopes of fitting into them again someday.

☐ On a rough day, your kids have eaten Goldfish crackers for breakfast, Oreos for lunch, and Frosted Flakes for dinner.

2–5 Points

You are probably a new mom who's wondering if she has what it takes to survive motherhood. At this point you may be thinking, *Who's Elmo, where's Dragon Land, and how long does an opera last anyway?*

6–10 Points

You have a couple of years' experience at this mothering gig and are starting to wonder when the raise kicks in…or at least when you can clock out and get some rest. I have bad news for you: There is no pay raise. In fact, there is no pay. And clocking out is not an option.

☐ The word *Yuck!* has officially been banned from your dinner table.

☐ You've fallen asleep sitting in a kitchen chair in the middle of lunch with tuna on your chin.

☐ Your social life consists of hanging out with other moms at McDonald's Playland, sipping soda.

☐ You only have time to shave one leg during your shower before someone screams, cries, or comes looking for you.

☐ Your child throws up, and you actually try to catch it in your hands.

☐ You catch yourself humming the *Elmo's World* theme song at dinner without even realizing you knew it by heart.

☐ You know who Arthur and Buster are, can count to ten in Spanish, and think that two-headed, fire-breathing dragons might make nice pets, if they could actually leave Dragon Land.

☐ If your minivan broke down in the middle of nowhere, you could

11 or More Points

You are the mom of all moms and have several years' experience under your belt (perhaps along with several added inches). You look forward to the day when your little angel goes off to kindergarten; this will finally give you time to paint your nails, take a long hot shower and shave *both* legs, and sip your morning coffee in peace and quiet. Of course, that's right about the time that little stick turns blue again, and you get a do-over with baby number two. Maybe this time you'll get it right![1]

Note to All Moms

Whether you are expecting your first baby or already have a dozen kids at home, *Rattled* is for you. This is because every time you have a baby, you must survive your baby's first year. You'll make new discoveries in *Rattled,* and you may even laugh out loud (making your husband think you have finally lost your mind, which is certainly better than losing your lunch).

You're ready to begin reading. And if you happen to fall asleep in the middle of a chapter, my feelings will not be hurt. I know how exhausting motherhood is.

Just try not to drool on the pages.

Beginning the Journey

Becoming a Mom

Star Light, Star Bright

Star light, star bright,
First star I see tonight,
Wish I may, wish I might,
Have the wish I wish tonight.

Mapping Out Motherhood

The First Three Trimesters

Water from the Word
*Your word is a lamp to my feet
and a light for my path.*
PSALM 119:105

Mike and I were married at twenty-three, fresh out of college, ready to take on the world. As newlyweds, we spent our evenings hand-washing dishes, talking about everything and nothing, and walking to the corner ice cream stand for a treat. We were happy, and we were in love. After a couple of years, we decided to try having a baby. And with that simple decision, our lives changed forever.

Plus Signs and Morning Sickness

When I make a decision, I expect things to happen immediately—if not sooner. Yep, I am a true control freak. So when Mike and I made the life-changing decision to have a baby, I thought I would get pregnant right away.

Imagine my shock when, after several months of trying, nothing happened. I grew more impatient by the day. I spent so much money on home pregnancy tests that I should have invested in e.p.t. I felt as though I had failed at motherhood before my journey had even begun.

After six months and no plus sign, I began to wonder if we were doing something wrong. That's when I jumped into action. I read everything I could get my hands on about how to get pregnant. Suddenly our romantic interludes involved basal thermometers, charts, calendars, and pillows stuffed here and there. I probably drove Mike crazy. But he was very patient with me, constantly reassuring me that it would happen in God's timing.

Problem was, I wanted it to happen in *my* timing.

Then, miracle upon miracle, in our eighth month of trying, that stubborn little stick produced a plus sign. We were going to have a baby.

What? We're having a baby?!

They always say to be careful what you wish for because you just might get it. Motherhood is definitely a living, breathing example of that. I had been working so hard to get pregnant that I hadn't taken much time to consider motherhood. That's when the nausea kicked in. Before I knew it, I'd lost control of my lunch—and my life.

Food for Thought

Women today are waiting until they are older to have their first baby. The birth rate for women ages 40 to 44 increased 81 percent between 1980 and 1995.[1]

Why are women waiting? Because Americans have seen a 50 percent increase in life expectancy over the last century. As a result, they're able to put off marriage and motherhood until later in life.

Buyer's Remorse

It's probably a good thing that most of us don't think through motherhood too carefully before we become pregnant. If we did, our species might completely die off. No one really considers what it will be like to gain forty pounds, get stretch marks in places you didn't think could stretch, increase an entire shoe size for good, or sacrifice a restful night's sleep for the next two decades.

Instead, all we think about is that precious little baby with twinkling eyes, peach fuzz for hair, dimples as deep as the Grand Canyon, and tiny little fingers and toes made just for kissing and tickling.

It's a case of bait and switch if ever I saw one, and there is no room here for buyer's remorse. Hospitals don't have a return or exchange policy. It's not like when you bought that pair of three-inch pumps that made your feet swell and could return them the next day for the flats that felt like butter. Nope. With a baby, you are in for life!

Basketballs, Watermelons, and MomQuest

I never was a petite gal—my mom calls it being "big-boned." I wanted to be built like Kelly Ripa, with stick legs and a waistline the size of most bangle bracelets. Instead, I was built more like a linebacker, with broad shoulders and muscular thighs. (Well, I like to think of them as muscular.)

So getting pregnant was the perfect reason to look the way I already looked and give purpose to my already existing belly. It also gave me an excuse to eat what I wanted and not count calories (not that I was counting calories to begin with). I no longer had to hold in my tummy; I was convinced that the little bulge around my middle was all baby (even though I was only six weeks pregnant). It felt like I'd won the "perfect excuse for having an out-of-shape body" lottery, and I was cashing in the check!

When I finally started to *look* pregnant, not as if I'd just put on a few pounds, I got excited. (Before that I considered wearing a name tag that read, HELLO, MY NAME IS TRISH. AND, NO, I'M NOT GAINING

WEIGHT FOR NO REASON. I'M ACTUALLY CARRYING ANOTHER HUMAN BEING IN MY BODY AT THE MOMENT. WHAT HAVE YOU DONE LATELY?)

Five months into pregnancy and I looked like I'd tucked a basketball under my shirt—all small and round, perfect and petite. That was during the second trimester, when life was good. The morning sickness was all but gone, the exhaustion had diminished, and I was truly enjoying the whole pregnancy experience. I had that euphoric feeling, that golden pregnancy glow, and was wearing those adorable little maternity overalls that make everyone want to touch your belly, even strangers.

But before I could really enjoy my little basketball-shaped tummy, it grew. And grew, and grew, and grew. It grew until it was more like a watermelon crammed under my shirt, lopsided and spilling over to my hips, chest, and thighs. I had entered the third trimester of my pregnancy and was fast approaching the need for a Wide Load sign and yellow flags hanging off my hips to warn people to step away as I approached.

That's when the wobbling began. No matter how hard I tried, I couldn't seem to walk straight. I wobbled left, then right, and then left again. I looked like an overweight, drunken sailor trying to walk a tightrope.

And everywhere I went, I needed to use the bathroom. With the baby sitting on my bladder, kicking my ribs every few seconds, I constantly had to pee. (Sorry if that word offends any of you. Having been a mom for over a decade now, bodily functions are a part of my daily lingo.)

Pretty soon I knew the location of every restroom in every public building within a twenty-mile radius. Just like MapQuest for expecting

---

Food for Thought

You know you're close to your due date when you no longer can fit into any maternity clothes and choose to instead hang out in your bathrobe at home, eating ice cream and thinking up creative ways to kick-start your labor.

moms—MomQuest! Just give me the location, and I'll tell you how to find the nearest restroom.

You say you're at JCPenney's lingerie department? (What in the world are you doing there? Don't you know breast milk stains silk?) Well, go three jogs left, down the long hallway to the main mall entrance, and head due south fifty paces. Shopping for baby clothes at The Children's Place? Their restroom is twenty paces left, three degrees due north. Stopping by Wal-Mart for some groceries? Forty steps inside the front door, then take a sharp left.

Football Games and Epidurals

One crisp autumn Friday in October 1995, I headed to a football game. Mike was the defensive coordinator for the Dalton Bulldogs high school football team, and every fall I spent Friday nights sitting in the bleachers cheering on the Bulldogs.

At eight and a half months pregnant, I feared that I would go into labor right there at the game and the announcer would make a scene getting Mike off the field: "Attention, ladies and gentlemen! Would Coach Mike Berg please report to the press box? Your wife has gone into labor." I didn't want to be the center of attention, at least not that way.

But I went to the game

Food for Thought

The normal length of pregnancy is from 37 to 41 weeks, with about 7 percent of all babies born at 42 weeks or later.[2]

Stage one of labor is from the time true labor begins until your cervix is dilated to 10 cm. Stage two is from the time your cervix is dilated to 10 cm until the baby is born.

For first-time moms, stage one lasts an average of 7.7 hours; stage two lasts an average of 53 minutes; and total labor lasts an average of 8.58 to 21.85 hours.[3]

anyway. I figured if I did go into labor, it was better to be near Mike than at home alone calling 911, because there was no way he was getting out of labor. Nope. He had to suffer right through the whole thing beside me, so I could numb his knuckles through every painful contraction.

After Dalton beat Northwestern that Friday night (I don't remember the score, but I'll bet Mike does), we went home and sank into bed, exhausted and drained. Around midnight, I began to roll over every hour or so like clockwork, just trying to get comfortable. I felt like a beached whale in a pile of sand. It wasn't pretty! And that's when my water broke, right there in bed. It shocked me so much that I moved faster than I had in months—I shot straight up. Mike, however, kept on dozing. It took me several minutes to wake him, let alone convince him that I was really in labor.

"Mike, I think my water just broke!"

"Trish, just go back to sleep. You have two weeks to go until your due date."

"Mike, I'm serious! Get up!"

"Let's wait a few hours and see, just to be sure. Try to go back to sleep."

Is he kidding?

Mike went back to snoring, and I started seething (and I'm oh-so-good at seething). Just when I was close to smacking him on the head, I decided there was a better solution. I simply took his hand and gently placed it in the puddle on the sheet.

That did it! He was up for good.

We called the hospital, and they told us to come in. Since I wasn't in any real pain yet, I decided to take a quick shower, shave my legs (the parts I could reach), and put some makeup on. I only wish I'd had time to give myself a pedicure, even though I couldn't reach my toes.

On the thirty-minute drive to the hospital, it started raining—a cold October rain that spit on the windshield. We were both so excited, so nervous…and so naive. The fact that my labor wasn't painful yet should have been the first clue that we were in for a very long haul.

And, yes, I did get an epidural. (I figured you'd want to know.) Initially, I was trying to go without one just to see if I could—that mom ego thing. That lasted until I was dilated to five centimeters. During one very painful contraction, with tears in my eyes I looked at Mike, and he said, "Trish, let's get the epidural."

Yeah! I am glad he helped me make that decision.

 ## Food for Thought

Depending on the size of the hospital, 40 percent to 70 percent of women use epidurals during labor.[4]

Ninety-one percent of women who planned to use an epidural during labor end up doing so.

Fifty-seven percent of women who hope to avoid using an epidural during labor end up using one to control pain.[5]

Epidurals provide complete relief for 85 percent of women, partial relief for 12 percent, and no relief at all for 3 percent.[6]

The epidural was a good thing for Mike as well. He didn't have to see me in pain, he could relax more, and I no longer squeezed his hand until his fingers turned blue. He also totally bonded with the anesthesiologist, who was a baseball umpire in his spare time. Dr. Bob Baab (no, I'm not kidding) and Mike formed an immediate friendship, which annoyed me at first. *I* was the patient; *I* was the one in pain. *I* should be getting all the attention!

But once the medication took effect and the mind-bending pain in my abdomen eased, it didn't bother me at all that they sat together in our room and watched the Ohio State Buckeyes play. Occasionally, Dr.

Baab would run out to check on another patient, but he was soon back to ask Mike what the score was and what he had missed (and he didn't mean the baby).

My labor lasted from morning to just past midnight. Mike and Bob even got to watch the Cleveland Indians in the playoffs that night. Yes, my labor was a reflection of my life: surrounded by sports, both on and off the field!

The Funny Thing About Epidurals

When I had my first child, I got what was called a walking epidural. It relieved pain but didn't completely numb my legs. When I explained this to my mom, she asked, "Trish, what is an epidural, anyway?" When she delivered my sister and me, there were no options. You gave birth, pain and all, or they knocked you out completely. So she was thrilled for me that I had a choice.

I ended up having epidurals with all four of my births. However, with my fourth child the epidural didn't work at all. (No, I'm not kidding. And, yes, it hurt like the dickens!) They inserted the needle, passed the fluid through, but there was no relief. My precious Riley was nine pounds, ten and a half ounces, and I felt every ounce during that delivery. I still joke that it was a good thing she wasn't our first baby, because she might have been an only child!

And no, I don't think women who go through natural childbirth are out of their minds. I'm simply thankful that women have choices today. Each and every one of you must make the decision you're comfortable with. Only you know your desires and limits. I have heard women who had cesareans say they felt cheated out of natural childbirth, as if they were deprived of something. Though I was never in their shoes, I can understand their disappointment.

I think my mom offers the best advice on this subject: "Keep your eye on the prize: a healthy baby and a healthy mom. Nothing else matters much after that."

 Food for Thought

WHERE DOES ALL THE WEIGHT GO?

The following is an approximate breakdown of your weight gain:

Baby = 7–8 pounds

Placenta = 1–2 pounds

Amniotic fluid = 2 pounds

Uterus = 2 pounds

Maternal breast tissue = 2 pounds

Maternal blood flow = 4 pounds

Fluids in maternal tissue = 4 pounds

Maternal fat and nutrient sources = 7 pounds

HOW MUCH TOTAL WEIGHT SHOULD I GAIN?

If you were a healthy weight before pregnancy, 25–37 pounds.

If you were underweight before pregnancy, 28–40 pounds.

If you were overweight before pregnancy, 15–25 pounds.[7]

FAITH ON FIRE

Dear Lord,

Thank You for loving me even more than I could ever fully imagine; for guiding my path and lighting a simple lamp unto my feet so I know where to walk; and for helping me to take the next step. Sometimes I want all the answers. I want You to shine a spotlight into my future, so I know what to expect at every turn and bump in the road. But, though I will never know what tomorrow holds, I do know that You hold tomor-

row in the palms of Your hands. Help me to find peace in that
and feel Your presence as I take that next step on the path You
are lighting for me.
In Jesus's name,
amen.

Shelter from the Storm

What surprised me the most was how I immediately
bonded with my baby. I felt an overwhelming and
complete love and devotion to this child.
—*ALLISON L.*

I was surprised that the pain after childbirth was
worse than the pain during childbirth.
—*SUSAN T.*

Don't expect the anesthesiologist or your obstetrician
to comment on how beautiful your legs are, even if you
did shave them after realizing you were in labor!
—*MELANIE M.*

I was surprised at how tender everything was, especially my breasts.
I was pregnant in the winter, and stepping out in the cold was
like poking a thousand needles into my chest.
—*ERIN S.*

When I arrived at the hospital, the doctor said,
"You're fully dilated. Let's get you in a room so you can start pushing."

"What about my epidural?" I balked. "We don't have time for that,"
he said. So I delivered with no drugs, no IV, no nothing.
Thirty minutes after I arrived, I had a baby in my arms.
And yes, it was painful, but it certainly was fast.

—JULIA B.

FIRST-AID KIT

Bring the following to the hospital.

For you

★ Your husband...don't forget him!

★ A soft cotton nightgown for after delivery (with nursing openings)

★ A warm robe; hospital rooms and hallways can get chilly

★ Socks or slippers to keep your feet warm

★ Maternity underwear (though the hospital may provide some)

★ Extra-long pads with wings (yes, you will need them for a while)

★ A toiletries bag containing soap, shampoo, a toothbrush, toothpaste, deodorant, mouthwash, a hairbrush, a blow-dryer, a curling iron, makeup—and anything else you'll need to feel pretty again

★ If possible, get a manicure and pedicure just before your delivery date. It will make you feel pretty and pampered when you need it the most. If money is tight, ask a girlfriend to give you one as a treat—then return the favor when she is due.

★ Breath mints, gum, or breath freshener

★ Your favorite sweet-smelling lotion

★ A list containing the phone numbers of everyone you want to call with the great news, along with a cell phone or prepaid long-distance calling card

★ A comfortable outfit to wear home from the hospital (and yes, it's perfectly fine to go home wearing maternity clothes)

★ A video camera and/or digital camera

★ Cash: bills and coins for the hospital vending machines and cafeteria, or to order takeout one night for you and your husband

★ Optional: If you have older children, it's nice to bring small, wrapped presents to give them when they visit you and their new brother or sister in the hospital. It removes any initial jealousy and makes the visit special for them as well.

For baby

☆ A receiving blanket to swaddle your baby in

☆ An outfit for your baby to wear home, including socks and cap

☆ A baby bunting or warm infant coat if it's cold outside

☆ An infant car seat for the drive home

☆ A pacifier, washed, in a zipper bag, and ready to use

Items to skip

◡ A silk nightgown that causes you to slip out of the bed and bruise your ego

◡ Strong perfume that makes your baby gag and the nurses avoid your room

◡ Your tight-fitting, prebaby jeans (they won't fit yet and will only depress you)

◡ Your Victoria's Secret lace bra that won't fit for a long time, if ever (besides, it will only get stained by breast milk)

◡ Books, cards, games, or any activity you think you might need to kill the time (any extra time will be spent sleeping!)

S.O.S.
(Spiritual Opportunity to Savor)

Immediately Jesus made the disciples get into the boat and go on ahead of him to the other side, while he dismissed the crowd. After he had dismissed them, he went up on a mountainside by himself to pray. When evening came, he was there alone, but the boat was already a considerable distance from land, buffeted by the waves because the wind was against it.

During the fourth watch of the night Jesus went out to them, walking on the lake. When the disciples saw him walking on the lake, they were terrified. "It's a ghost," they said, and cried out in fear.

But Jesus immediately said to them: "Take courage! It is I. Don't be afraid."

"Lord, if it's you," Peter replied, "tell me to come to you on the water."

"Come," he said.

Then Peter got down out of the boat, walked on the water and came toward Jesus. But when he saw the wind, he was afraid and, beginning to sink, cried out, "Lord, save me!"

Immediately Jesus reached out his hand and caught him. "You of little faith," he said, "why did you doubt?"

And when they climbed into the boat, the wind died down. Then those who were in the boat worshiped him, saying, "Truly you are the Son of God."

MATTHEW 14:22–33

The Faith Walk of a Mom

It recently occurred to me that this story is a lot like motherhood. Having a baby is a leap of faith, a walking-on-water experience in which we have to trust God for the outcome. We take tiny little steps out onto the water, tiptoeing through the shallow end.

But God wants us to know that He is there waiting for us to leap in. He will catch us. When our faith falters as Peter's did and we begin to sink, God is there to grab hold and pull us up. What an amazing God we follow. We can trust Him that for each step we take, each day we face, He is there with His hand outstretched to catch us if we begin to sink in our human frailty.

Study Questions

1. At the beginning of this story, Jesus sends the disciples away and goes alone to the mountainside to pray—in peace, in quiet. In the midst of His ministry, Jesus took some time for Himself to seek God. When was the last time you did that? How can you make time every day to pray in peace and quiet?

2. Can you think of a time in your life when you faltered in your faith, when you felt like you were sinking as Peter did? Did you feel God grab hold and pull you up? How did God show you mercy?

3. How can you show that same mercy to others?

Gearing Up for the Journey

The Fourth Trimester

Water from the Word

I lie down and sleep; I wake again,
because the LORD sustains me.

PSALM 3:5

There is a place from which there is no return and no escape, a place where you will question everything. A place where you'll make mistakes—tons of them. Worse, you'll never know if you got it right until several decades have passed and it's too late for improvement. It will be the most painful and joyful place you ever visit.

Only you don't *visit* this place; you live there. It's called the fourth trimester.

As a mother, you'll enter the fourth trimester when your first child is born. It doesn't matter whether you've given birth or adopted a child; he is your baby. And he will change the very essence of who you are.

Entering the fourth trimester means stepping into a new reality. When your little baby cries for the first time, your heart becomes one with his. Your eyes see the world in a new light. After all, you are *completely responsible for the life and well-being of another human.* (If you've now entered a state of panic, do the following: take a deep breath, lower your shoulders, and tell yourself that you are not alone.)

One Trimester at a Time

Whether your pregnancy was planned or not, that first trimester often sneaks up on you. The little stick turns blue, your heart skips a beat, and you think, *Wow, a baby!* Then the morning sickness hits, accompanied by complete exhaustion…and you begin wondering if you'll survive the next two months.

The second trimester brings about welcome change. You can finally tell your friends you're pregnant—and even better, you actually *look* pregnant rather than just chunky. You buy some maternity clothes and begin to plan your nursery decorations and theme. (Of course, you have to have a theme; it's in the rule book.)

The third trimester sneaks up on you, and before you know it, you've traded in that early pregnancy glow for a waddle walk and swollen feet. The good news is that you begin to feel the reality of having a baby. You can hardly wait to meet your precious little one. You dream about her perfect blue eyes, pink cheeks, and itty-bitty fingers and toes. You hang color-coordinated Noah's Ark wallpaper in your nursery and spend way too much money on a matching crib quilt set (which you won't be able to use, since you can't put blankets or pillows in a crib).

Sometimes you accidentally bump your pregnant belly into the countertop while reaching for a glass. You may knock over a lamp in the family room. Your back aches, your knees buckle, you limp and waddle when you walk, and you haven't seen your feet in weeks. You sleep in hour-long intervals. Turning over in bed becomes a chore equivalent to rolling a boulder uphill on a sheet of ice.

Your due date is written on the calendar in ink, as if its permanent nature will help make it happen. (You even underline it three times, just for emphasis.) You feel like you have been pregnant for two years. You only have one maternity shirt left that actually covers your belly. You know what lies ahead—or at least you think you do. After three trimesters of pregnancy, you are ready for the end.

But the fourth trimester is not just an end to pregnancy; it is the beginning of a lifelong adventure. The first year of motherhood is definitely the most life-altering, exhausting, and exciting.

Reality Check

The day I got a good dose of reality, I was eight months pregnant and standing in line at the grocery store. My back ached, my feet throbbed, and I wondered idly to myself when this baby would ever come so I could feel better.

Then it hit me. *Once the baby is born, my life will never be normal again.*

To my credit, I didn't pass out, scream, pant, or bang my head into the cart. On the outside, I probably looked quite normal. But inside I was in a complete panic about becoming a mom.

Food for Thought

Multiples are on the rise. Of all live births in the United States in 2004, 3.4 percent were multiple births. The multiple birth ratio in the United States increased 32 percent between 1994 and 2004.[1]

Not long after my reality check at the grocery store, it also sank in for Mike. As I snuggled down one night for my usual one hour of straight sleep (before the bathroom sprints began), he turned to me in panic and said, "Trish, I'm not sure I'm ready to be a dad."

Now my panic attack was poised to become a full-fledged nervous breakdown! If I didn't know what I was doing and Mike didn't know what he was doing, how in the world were the two of us going to raise this baby? This was the question that haunted me as I rolled over and closed my eyes in an attempt to avoid saying, "I'm not sure I'm ready to be a mom!"

I'd spent so much time preparing for the baby's birth that I didn't think about something important: pregnancy is only the beginning. It's a starting place, not an ending. Sure, you stop being pregnant after three trimesters…but the birth of your child doesn't signal the end of anything. Rather, it is the beginning of motherhood. An entrance, not an exit. No one had told me that, and it really took me by surprise.

Ticket, Please

Motherhood is a lot like riding a roller coaster: You hold on tight, let out a few screams, and treasure each twist and turn along the way.

I actually entered my fourth trimester fairly easily. My delivery went well, though my labor was long. (Hard labor lasted for exactly fifteen and a half hours, but who's counting?) And then there she was: Hannah Kathryn Berg, born October 15, 1995. Life as I knew it would never be the same again. When I saw her little pout and her beautiful eyes, when she grabbed my finger and nursed at my breast, nothing else mattered.

I was on the verge of an adventure, the kind about which novels are written. The kind where there is a surprise around every turn. Let it be noted that the fourth trimester is *filled* with change. After all, once you are a mom, you are a mom for life. There is no GET OUT OF MOTHERHOOD FREE card. The stakes are high. Moms are expected to move smoothly down the time line, from crib to college, and not miss a beat along the way.

Beginning the Journey in Style

Hannah was a perfect baby—definitely a keeper. However, she developed a severe case of jaundice the day after she was born, which meant that we had to spend two extra days at the hospital. By day four, I was ready to go home. I wanted to sleep in my own bed, tuck Hannah into her dainty bassinet, and get back to the real world. On day five, we were allowed to leave.

Now, I have to preface what happened next by telling you that Mike isn't known for surprising me. He is a romantic, but he has truly surprised me only a few times in our marriage. He didn't surprise me when he proposed, because we picked out the ring together. We planned our honeymoon together, so no surprises there.

The fact is, I like it that way. We are a team. But gals, you and I both know that it's wonderful to be romanced once in a while—surprised, knocked off our feet by our sweethearts. We want to be the princess swept away by our knight in shining armor on a white stallion.

So when the nurse wheeled me out of the hospital that day, tears welled up in my eyes. I couldn't believe the mode of transportation Mike had lined up for us. My Prince Charming may not have ridden up on a white horse to rescue me, but he did rent a white stretch limo to carry me home. I felt like a princess. It was the perfect beginning to our lives as parents.

Ignorance Is Bliss

As we rode home in luxury, I smiled and thought to myself, *We're ready. We can handle this parenting thing.* We had it all figured out. We had built up a little bit of parenting confidence at the hospital by successfully bathing and diapering Hannah. Nursing was going well, and she was already sleeping for several hours at a stretch.

Food, clean pants, and baths. What more does a baby need, right? At that moment in time, I was pretty blissful about motherhood. But, like *Fantasy Island,* the dream can only last so long. We were about to get hit smack-dab in the face with the hard, cold reality of life with a newborn.

Let's face it. When you bring your first baby home from the hospital, you're totally focused on the moment. Thinking about the future?

🍼 *Food for Thought*

Most newborn babies average 16 hours of sleep each day, but as any mom will tell you, never more than a few hours at a time. Most three- to four-month-old babies will sleep consistently through the night.

To help your baby sleep through the night, don't play or socialize with her during night wakings. Keep the room dimly lit, feed and change her quietly, and then put her back down.[2]

Ha! I couldn't think beyond the next five minutes.

Everything happened fast and seemed very exciting. We were greeted at our home by a wealth of family and friends, all there to meet Hannah. Someone had prepared dinner for us, and plenty of hugs and kisses gave us a sense of love and family. Everyone oohed and aahed over Hannah. It was our fifteen minutes of fame, and we savored every moment of it.

Then everyone left and there we were with Hannah, who looked up at us like we should know what to do with her. That's when the panic set in. Suddenly I wasn't sure we would make it through our first night as parents, let alone survive the next twenty years.

After my initial terror subsided and my heart began to beat at less than light speed, I looked at my adoring husband. *Okay,* I thought. *It's up to us. We're adults. We've prepared for this moment. We can do it!* Our plan was to get settled in, put Hannah to sleep in her bassinet, and go to bed. We were both so exhausted (bringing a new life into the world wears you out).

Like many first-time parents before us, we were a bit too optimistic. Looking back, I realize I should have asked some of those adoring relatives to hang around a bit longer and take turns walking the floor with Hannah that night. Maybe then we could have slept. As it turned out, Hannah did not sleep at all her first night home. Not one wink. Not one snore. Not unless she was cuddled in our arms and we were bouncing her up and down as we paced the floor.

So Mike and I took turns walking laps around the house, bouncing her to some imaginary music in our heads (probably hallucinating due to lack of sleep). I think we wore a hole in the carpet that night: around the kitchen table, through the family room, around the corner into the living room, and back to the kitchen. It was like the Daytona 500 without the speed (and a lot more bouncing).

Some laps were sleepwalked. But praise the Lord, we didn't fall down or drop her, so I guess we were semiconscious. When the walker tired, he or she would pass the baby off to the couch sleeper to take a turn. Like a tag-team relay, we spent the night grabbing twenty-minute naps in between laps. It was a true test of stamina, teamwork, and marital strength.

I missed the hospital nursery and all of the help we had there. I even considered driving back to see if they would take Hannah for a few hours. I thought, *What were we thinking, having a baby? We don't know what we're doing. We may never sleep again!* That's when the tears began to flow. I sobbed to Mike, "Is this what we've signed up for? Will the rest of our lives be sleepless?"

Working the Third Shift

As the days went on (or nights—I couldn't tell the difference anymore), I eventually lost my night-shift partner. Mike had to start sleeping at night so he could go to work in the mornings.

That was when I discovered the blessings of working the third shift.

When Mike came home from work, he would take Hannah (actually, I shoved her in his arms), and I would run upstairs, lock the bedroom door, and sleep for three or four straight hours. It was like heaven to be able to crawl under the soft blankets and know that I was off duty.

Food for Thought

Americans aren't sleeping enough.

Adults need seven to nine hours of sleep (in a row) each night to function well, yet 39 percent get less than seven hours of sleep each weeknight. About three-quarters (74 percent) of American adults regularly experience a sleeping problem a few nights a week. More than one in three (37 percent) say lack of sleep interferes with daily activities.[3]

Around 9 p.m. I would get up, shower, blow-dry my hair, and sometimes even apply makeup just to feel human again. Then I would grab a quick snack, drink an ice-cold glass of water, and get ready for the night shift. At this point Mike would pass Hannah to me and go to bed.

Mike and I didn't see each other much during Hannah's first few months of life. But taking shifts with Hannah allowed us to get some rest, and as much as I missed spending time with Mike in the evenings, I needed the sleep more.

Accepting that I had to be up all night helped my sanity and allowed me to actually enjoy those hours with Hannah. I turned on all the lights downstairs so that I could think of it as daytime. I grew very familiar with the lineup of late-night shows on television (not many were good, but they kept me company). I learned that they replayed the news at 2 a.m. and that *Oprah* came on at 3 a.m.

Hannah and I spent the first few months of her life hanging out together in the family room all night long. During those slumber parties I ate supper at midnight and breakfast at 4 a.m. Hannah usually slept for a few solid hours from 5 a.m. to 8 a.m., so I took advantage of that and rested as well.

When she was three months old, Hannah started sleeping better. She got up only twice, around midnight and 4 a.m., to eat. I could depend on three to four hours of sleep in a row. I finally wore pajamas again and slept in my own bed! Let me tell you, our old mattress never felt so good.

The Battle of the Breast

Before I attended childbirth classes while pregnant with Hannah, I knew virtually nothing about breast-feeding. The biggest surprise was that breast-feeding isn't an innate act. I had to teach my baby to latch on correctly, and I had to learn how to hold Hannah so she could feed comfortably without getting gas.

Back in the sixties when I was a baby, most medical advice discouraged breast-feeding and promoted formula as the best source of nutrition for babies. Society has come full circle with the "breast is best" campaign, which puts pressure on moms from all walks of life to breast-feed their babies. (Boy, new moms sure do carry the weight of the world on their shoulders.)

The American Academy of Pediatrics recommends that moms breast-feed if possible, especially during the first four months of the baby's life. And if a mother can breast-feed her baby for the entire first year, it's even better.

I enjoyed breast-feeding all four of my children, usually weaning them sometime prior to their first birthday. But Mike and I also supplemented with formula, which allowed me the freedom to be gone for more than two hours at a stretch. This can provide a much-needed break for an exhausted mom.

Weigh all your options before you decide what to do. If your desire is to breast-feed, I think that's wonderful. But if you can't for any reason, please don't feel guilty. The formulas available on the market today are nutritious and give babies plenty of what they need.

Food for Thought
Research has shown that for every year a woman breast-feeds her baby, her risk of developing breast cancer might be reduced by 4.3 percent. Women who give birth to more children are also less likely to develop breast cancer than women who give birth to fewer children. The risk of breast cancer declines by 7 percent for every child a woman has birthed.[4]

My adventures in nursing went smoothly with Hannah, but I developed a breast infection when Sydney, our second daughter, was a baby. To give you an idea of just how painful this condition is, imagine the worst breast pain you have ever felt and top it off with flulike symptoms that include a fever and the chills...and you're halfway there. Once I was on antibiotics, however, the symptoms subsided and I was able to continue nursing.

By the time Colin and Riley were born, I had the breast-feeding thing down pat. I could nurse anywhere, anytime. I carried a nursing bib in my diaper bag that strapped around my neck and covered both baby and breast. I nursed my babies in malls, restaurants, sitting in my parked car, at football and baseball games, and even in the middle of the zoo. It became second nature.

Once my babies reached about ten months, I was ready to wean them. There just comes a time when you want your body back. I had rented it out for nine months of pregnancy, after all, followed by ten months of feeding on demand. Besides, I'd gotten tired of my breasts being as big as footballs and as heavy as anchors. I was also tired of nursing bras that were about as sexy as body armor. And I think I leaked on every blouse I owned.

Food for Thought

In 2001, 65.1 percent of moms breast-fed their babies in the hospital, but only 27 percent were still nursing their six-month-old, and only 12.3 percent made it to their baby's first birthday.

In 2003, 70.9 percent of moms breast-fed their babies in the hospital, but only 36.2 percent were still nursing their six-month-old, and 17.2 percent made it to their baby's first birthday.

The U.S. Centers for Disease Control and Prevention's goal for 2010 is that 75 percent of moms nurse their babies in the hospital, 50 percent make it through six months, and 25 percent nurse during the entire first year of motherhood.[5]

But I have to admit that the biggest incentive for me to wean my babies was when allergy season arrived. I have severe springtime allergies, and as long as I was pregnant or nursing, I couldn't take any allergy medicine. As a result, my eyes swelled shut every morning, I sneezed uncontrollably, and I was stuffed up and congested from head to toe. So when the month of May came around, if my babies were more than ten months old, it was time for me to wean them.

I know that breast-feeding is your decision to make, and you will surely be bombarded with opinions about what is best for you and for your baby. Keep in mind that whether you breast-feed or not, your baby will be nourished by a lot more than just the milk you feed him. He will be nourished by your love.

Food for Thought

TOP FIVE BENEFITS OF BOTTLE-FEEDING

1. You know exactly how much milk your baby is getting.

2. Dad, siblings, and grandparents can take part in feeding your baby, giving you more freedom. This also allows other family members to bond with the baby.

3. Hubby can help with nighttime feedings, letting you get more hours of continuous sleep.

4. Unlike a breast-feeding mother, you can use whatever kind of birth control you choose, and you don't have to carefully watch what you eat. Six weeks after delivery you can start to diet and exercise to lose weight.

5. Your body is yours once again.[6]

TOP FIVE BENEFITS OF BREAST-FEEDING

1. You have readily available nourishment for your baby on demand, whenever your baby wants it and wherever you are.

2. Breast milk is free. Exclusively nursing could save you over $1,200 by the time your baby is a year old.

3. Your baby gets the best nutrition possible from your breast milk, including antibodies and immune boosts.

4. Breast-feeding burns tons of calories and shrinks your uterus more quickly, helping you get back to your prepregnancy weight.

5. It may reduce your risk of breast cancer.[7]

FAITH ON FIRE

Dear Lord,

Thank You for this precious baby, this glimpse of heaven, this gift from You. Help me remember that as much as I love him, You love him even more. It is scary not knowing what tomor-

row holds for my child or for me, but I know that You are
with me through it all. I can't begin to imagine the life You
have in store for my baby, but I'm blessed to be along for the
ride. Help me to love You and turn to You for guidance, grace,
and forgiveness.

In Jesus's name,

amen.

Shelter from the Storm

*When my first child was born, I remember being up for those
late-night feedings, looking out the window into the darkness,
and feeling totally overwhelmed and sad that I wasn't in bed asleep.*

—LISA G.

*My daughter, Sheryle, was constantly worrying about her newborn's
weight gain. By then her milk had come in, her breasts were
regulation-size NFL footballs, and the baby seemed satisfied.
But new moms worry. So after church, I took her to the store and
we went straight to the produce section. When no one was looking,
we laid Jack gently in the vegetable weight bin, suspended by a
shiny silver chain. Jack checked in about the size of a small melon.
To Sheryle's delight, he'd gained back the weight he lost in the
hospital plus another six ounces. We gathered up our little seven-
pound bundle, bought a loaf of bread, and Sheryle floated
out of the store, a confident new mother.*

—CATHY M.

*My husband and I tag-teamed the nighttime routine.
Once the twins settled into getting up only a couple of times a night,*

I would do the weeknights and my husband would do the
weekends so I could catch up on my sleep.

—VICKIE S.

Our baby girl always turned her face to light, whether it was
sunshine or a lamp. We worried that it might ruin her eyes,
so at her six-week checkup, we asked her doctor. He looked at us with
a quirky smile and said, "If it bothers her eyes, she'll shut them."
We didn't ask him any other silly questions!

—MIRIAM K.

The hardest part for me was "getting my mommy legs." You know,
adjusting to the constant shifts of motherhood: coordination to whip out
the "meals on wheels" and nurse impromptu, or balancing the diaper bag
and the baby carrier while trying to open car doors or load groceries.

—ERIN S.

FIRST-AID KIT

☆ **Wisdom.** Don't underestimate the value of wisdom from your mom or mother-in-law. Take them up on the help they offer and listen to their advice. Even if you don't choose to follow it, listening shows them respect and love.

☆ **Meals.** When people offer to bring you a meal, *say yes*—always! If you are not ready for company, be honest with them; ask if they can drop the meal off now and plan a visit down the road when you are more settled in. But never turn away food during those first few months.

☆ **Memories.** When your child is a newborn, dress him in an outfit that is far too big for him at that time and take pictures of him in it once a month. Through this series of images, you can watch your child grow into his clothes as you mark his growth!

☆ **Cleaning.** If you can afford it, hire a housecleaner for the first year. Even having someone come once a month will help keep your house clean and your sanity intact. If money is tight, ask a girlfriend to help you out. It will make her feel needed and appreciated, and you can return the favor when *she* needs one.

☆ **Crying.** When you've hit your limit, are exhausted, and the baby is crying, don't be afraid to cry with him. When nothing you do is settling him down, just sit in a chair, hold him, and cry with him. It helps.

☆ **Sleep.** The best advice for new moms? Sleep when the baby sleeps. The worst advice? Sleep when the baby sleeps. It's about balance, so do what works for you.

☆ **Baby blues.** If you feel extremely overwhelmed, have trouble sleeping, lose your appetite, cry frequently, don't feel happy, and don't want to participate in your normal activities, see your doctor right away. You might have postpartum depression, and there is medication available that will help.

☆ **Breast-feeding.** If you breast-feed, always pour a big glass of water for yourself when you sit down to nurse. As the baby drinks, you drink as well; when she is done, you should have an empty glass. It helps keep you hydrated so you always have enough milk for your baby.

S.O.S.
(SPIRITUAL OPPORTUNITY TO SAVOR)

Jesus sat down opposite the place where the offerings were put and watched the crowd putting their money into the temple treasury. Many rich people threw in large amounts. But a poor widow came and put in two very small copper coins, worth only a fraction of a penny.

Calling his disciples to him, Jesus said, "I tell you the truth, this poor widow has put more into the treasury than all the others. They all gave out of their wealth; but she, out of her poverty, put in everything—all she had to live on."

MARK 12:41–44

 ## Giving More Than I Have

I have been a mom for over a decade now, yet every day I struggle with giving every last ounce of energy to my kids. There are some days—most, actually—when I feel completely drained.

Being a mom is downright exhausting. You are basically called to give more than you have energywise, lovewise, timewise, and hopewise. Your newborn baby has so many needs, and you are the one there to meet those needs every hour of every day. It can wear you out.

But God is bigger than our exhaustion; He can sustain us. We have to seek Him and be willing to let others help us.

There's a funny story you've probably heard about a guy whose city is flooding. Being a faithful Christian, he climbs to the roof of his house and waits for God to save him.

Soon a boat comes by, and a rescue worker invites him to jump on board.

"No," the man says. "God will save me."

Then a helicopter flies by, and the pilot offers him a ride.

"No thanks," he says. "God will save me."

Pretty soon the floodwaters overtake the poor man's house, and he dies. When he gets to heaven, he tells God, "I waited for You! Why didn't You save me?"

God replies, "I sent a boat and a helicopter. What more did you want?"

This story illustrates how many ways God sends us help. A mother-in-law who offers to come and baby-sit for an afternoon. A neighbor who cooks you supper. A friend who watches the baby for an hour so you can nap. A husband who wants to help but changes the diapers wrong and has no idea how to feed the baby properly.

As moms, we need to accept the help God sends and be thankful for His tiny miracles, *not* wait for a BIG miracle that we're certain is just around the corner.

Study Questions

1. In what ways do you feel as if you are giving more than you have to this precious baby?
2. Has someone in your life offered to help you out? Have you turned her down?
3. What are some baby steps you can take toward either allowing others to help you or asking for help when you need it?

Changing Seasons

Losing Sleep

I See the Moon

I see the moon and the moon sees me,
The moon sees somebody I'd like to see.
God bless the moon and God bless me.
God bless the one I love.

I really think the Lord above,
Created you for me to love.
He picked you out from all the rest,
Because He knew I'd love you best.

When I get to heaven and you're not there,
I'll write your name on the golden stair.
I'll write it big so the angels can see,
Just how much you mean to me.

Survival Mode

Life with a Baby in the House

Water from the Word
The LORD says: … "As a mother comforts her child,
so will I comfort you."
ISAIAH 66:12–13

During those first few months of motherhood, when the exhaustion was overwhelming, I learned to live in survival mode. Survival mode is when you can provide only the bare necessities, the basic needs of life: food, shelter, water, clothing. You feed your baby, change dirty diapers, maybe get a few cookies stuffed in your mouth at 3 a.m. Pajamas or sweatpants are the wardrobe of choice, and just forget about showering before noon.

During my early days in survival mode, Mike frequently arrived home from work to find me just as he left me: still in pajamas, my hair a mess, clothes and toys everywhere, diapers (both dirty and clean) stacked on the coffee table, and wearing an expression of such deep exhaustion that it made him tired simply looking at me.

He would give me a big hug and say, "How was your day, honey?" When I handed over our slobbery, crying, and oftentimes poopy baby, he simply kissed my forehead and took over while I ran upstairs for a much-needed nap. (Yes, I married the right man!)

Survival mode became a way of life for us during those early months of parenting. In fact, we spent so much time living in survival mode, we probably should have sent out change of address cards to our family and friends so they knew where to find us. I remember the overwhelming realization that I might never sleep through the night again. Since Hannah had her days and nights backward, it was like working a third-shift job minus the benefit of clocking out at dawn.

The most amazing thing was that once Hannah was three months old, her improved sleep pattern had as much to do with our parenting development as her own infant development. (As with many parenting breakthroughs, it is often the parents who benefit most from the lesson, not the child.) Once Hannah was old enough, we found out that we *needed* to let her cry it out. I guess it was the first time we realized that we couldn't fix all her problems. You might even say it was the first step in letting Hannah go, a process that hasn't let up since. Sometimes I catch a glimpse of my beautiful twelve-year-old daughter and wonder just where that pudgy-cheeked baby went.

I spent many sleepless nights during those first few months of Hannah's life. So you can imagine what a shock it was when our second child, Sydney, slept four to five hours a night in her own crib from the moment we brought her home from the hospital. Colin, born two years later, was a great sleeper right from the start as well. I smugly thought, *It must be me!* Clearly, I had become a much more relaxed mom since having Hannah. I quickly patted myself on the back and chalked one up for mom.

Needless to say, I was a *little* too quick to credit myself for their sleeping success. Enter my daughter Riley, our youngest and last. From the beginning, Riley didn't want to sleep in her bassinet or the crib. She didn't like the cradle or even the swing. In fact, the only place she wanted to sleep was on me—right smack-dab on top of my chest. (It made for easy nursing access, I suppose.)

Oh, I tried, night after night, to put her to bed somewhere, anywhere other than on me. But each time she would sleep for only twenty minutes and wake up screaming. It was so exhausting and completely frustrating. So I resorted to what worked, as moms do sometimes. Every night after Mike and the older kids went to bed, I plopped myself on the recliner with pillows stuffed under my arms. I nursed Riley, and we slept there together all night. And as much as I didn't like sleeping in a semi-upright position, Riley would sleep four to five hours in a row on me, so it was the best option for me at that time to get any sleep at all.

As for the sleeping score (in case you're keeping track), it's kids 4, mom 0. I realized through that experience that Sydney and Colin were easy sleepers not because of anything I did; rather, it was because they came that way—it was how God made them. I couldn't take credit at all.

When I took Riley in for her one-week checkup, I asked her pediatrician, Dr. Strong, if I could just put her down and let her cry. He informed me that Riley was too young to let cry. Essentially, he said I should do whatever I needed to survive her first three months. After that, we could discuss working with Riley on sleeping better at night.

Do whatever I needed to survive, huh? Well, I did survive those three months.

Then came Riley's three-month checkup. I was giddy as a schoolgirl with a crush, knowing I could finally sleep in my own bed that night. I greeted Dr. Strong with a smile, and he quickly assured me that it was time to try a sleep routine with Riley. After explaining what I should do, he noted that for the first few nights his name would be mud around our house, because Riley would probably cry a lot. But he also assured me that if I stuck with the routine, Mike and I would praise his name once again.

He was right—it took Riley only three nights to develop a great sleep pattern. And with that, I returned to my own bed.

Transition to Baby Mode

Eventually, survival mode leads to baby mode. Your entire world becomes stuffed with feeding schedules, napping times, formula mixes, baby food jars, rattles, bouncy seats, swings, and playpens. And that's just a short list of the clutter in your house and your life while you're in baby mode!

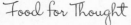 Food for Thought

THE SLEEP PROGRAM THAT WORKED FOR ME*

1. Decide what time you want to put your baby to bed. Any time will work, but it needs to be same time every night. Routine consistency is extremely important.

2. When the predetermined time draws near, give your baby a warm bath while talking and singing to her softly. Babies aren't dirty enough to need a bath every night, of course; but this soothing routine will signal that it's time to wind down and go to sleep.

3. After your baby's bath, wrap him in a towel, then diaper, dress, and feed him in the nursery with no one else around. Keep the lights and noise low. Speak in whispers and lullabies.

4. Next comes bedtime. Choose a ritual you are comfortable with—you can feed, rock, then lay her in the crib; or you can feed her and then read a book. The elements of the routine don't matter, so long as they are the same every night.

5. When your baby is ready for bed, gently lay him in the crib. (Don't worry about whether he is asleep or awake.)

Hannah loved one specific clown toy. It was plastic, too big to swallow but small enough to fit in her mouth. Well, part of it. She would stick that clown headfirst in her mouth and crawl around the house. We used to call her Clown Mouth, and though we never quite figured out why she liked the toy, we knew we had to have it on hand everywhere we went. Baby mode.

Sydney was a pacifier baby. She needed her pacifier to soothe her fears and tears. So I bought cases of pacifiers and kept them in every nook and cranny of our home and car. I handed them out to grandparents and neighbors so that no matter where we were, there would be a pacifier handy. Baby mode.

---

6. Stroke her head or tummy several times and whisper a few comforting words, such as "Night-night, sweetheart. Mommy loves you." Again, what you say is not as important as saying the same thing every night.

7. Leave the room (the hardest part). Your baby may fall asleep immediately, or he may awaken and begin to cry.

8. If she does cry, let her do so for ten to fifteen minutes. Then quietly go back in, stroke her on the tummy or head, repeat your night-night phrase, and leave again. (Don't pick up your baby; it will stimulate and awaken her even more.)

9. Repeat the above step until he is sound asleep. The first few nights will be the hardest, but each night he will get better at self-soothing. Eventually he will become a great sleeper, and you will have your nights back again.

* Some pediatricians recommend waiting until the baby is six months old before letting her cry it out; others say three months is plenty. Be sure to check with your pediatrician before implementing any sleep system to make sure it is healthy for your baby.

Colin was a thumbsucker. But the kicker was that he had a soft fleece blanket with silky edging that he held in the palm of his hand as he sucked his thumb. He slept with that blanket every night and carried it all over the house. I was so afraid we would lose it that I went to a fabric store, bought a yard or two of soft fleece, and cut up eight-inch squares to imitate the blanket. I also learned to wash his actual blanket and those squares at the same time, in the same load, so they would smell identical. I had blanket squares stuffed in the diaper bag, my purse, and the minivan's glove compartment. Baby mode.

By the time Riley arrived, I already had three active children running around the house. My biggest fear with her was that she would choke on a Barbie shoe or race car. And we lived in a gated community—baby-gated. I gated off the staircase, the living room, and the basement. Baby mode.

Food for Thought

THE BEST-KEPT SURVIVAL MODE SECRETS

Let Daddy pitch in. Take turns with your husband doing bathing and bedtime routines. That way each of you gets a break, and each of you gets time to bond with baby.

Go light on gear. Most moms find they don't need all that stuff, from bouncy seats to backpack carriers. Start simple. You can always add gear down the road, borrow it from a friend, or find it inexpensively at a garage sale.

Make meals simple. There is nothing wrong with feeding your baby sliced chicken nuggets for lunch. Add a sliced banana and some cheese. It's a good meal.

Forgo the fancy wardrobe. Kids get dirty, spit up, and spill juice on themselves. Keep their wardrobe simple and inexpensive. Shop Goodwill and garage sales, or accept clothes from friends whose kids are older than yours.

I also discovered that sometimes the world works better in reverse. Instead of putting Riley in her playpen to play, which sometimes made her cry, I placed three-year-old Colin in there with his Matchbox cars and building blocks. Riley loved roaming the house, and Colin acted like he had entered paradise, sitting in the coveted spot, a place that was usually off-limits to him. Baby mode!

Hannah loved the doorway jumper that hung between the kitchen and family room—she would jump and swing so high that we finally had to take it down for fear she would catapult herself into next week. Sydney loved the rolling activity center, and Colin loved the vibrating bouncy seat. I discovered that each of my children had their own likes and dislikes as infants, and it didn't take long to figure out what made them happy.

In the long run, I got my "mom legs"—the ability to balance a toddler on one hip, hoist a diaper bag over one shoulder, carry a car seat

---

Enjoy tub time. If you play with your baby while she's in the tub, she will come to love bath time. And don't be afraid of getting water in her face. Your anxiety about it could translate into fussiness later.

Tune out tantrums. Don't get angry, upset, or excited when your baby throws a tantrum. Keep your cool. As long as he is safe, just walk away. The more you ignore tantrums, the faster they will go away.

Trust your instincts. Accept other people's maternal advice with grace—and a grain of salt. When they comment negatively on your baby's eating or napping habits, thank them for their input; but ultimately, trust your own instincts.

Don't let a schedule hold you prisoner. As much as babies love a regular schedule, it does tie you to the house. When you are home, follow that schedule. But remember that babies are adaptable—they can nap in the car or nurse wherever you want them to. So don't stop living. Get out and go![1]

in the other hand, and not trip or drop anything. I learned to relax and simply have fun with my kids at every age.

Through it all, I discovered that living in baby mode didn't mean giving up my previous life. It just meant adapting my life to meet my kids' needs. Well worth the effort, with eternal blessings.

Rediscovering the World

Once your newborn begins sleeping through the night, you will rediscover a bright, sunshiny world out there waiting just for you. You can get up in the morning and actually shower and dress sometime before noon. If you feel brave, you might even plan a trip to a friend's house, the mall, or the grocery store. Most baby-on-hip activities will depend on whether this is your first baby or whether you're a veteran mom.

When Hannah was born, our then-pediatrician told us we shouldn't

---

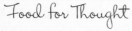

Food for Thought

FIVE WAYS TO BE A GREAT DAD

1. **Bedtime.** Take over the baby bedtime routine, from bath time to bedtime books. This will allow you bonding time with baby and give your wife a needed break.

2. **Feedings.** On the weekends, take some of the late-night bottle-feeding shifts to allow your wife a few extra hours of sleep.

3. **Diapers.** Jump in and change those diapers. Don't worry about doing it perfectly; just do it.

4. **Time out.** Encourage your wife to go for a baby-free walk after dinner or out for coffee with friends.

5. **Romance.** Don't forget to romance your wife. Buy her flowers, take her out to dinner, and make dates with her again. She was your wife before the baby was born, and she'll be your wife long after your children grow up.

take her out in public for three months except to our parents' homes. Initially, his advice sounded good to me. I wasn't *ready* to go out with her; I was terrified that germs were just waiting to jump and land in her face.

But need I remind you how long three months is? When Hannah was about six weeks old, I began to feel trapped. It was like being confined in a prison with gingham couches and wallpaper.

To our credit, we listened to our doctor. She was our first baby, and I was suffering from first-time-mom syndrome. But we eventually relaxed a bit and began taking Hannah to quiet places with family, like out to eat on a Saturday night with Mike's parents.

Making Those Mommy Mistakes

When Hannah was about two months old, she slept for a good hour after every nursing. So one evening we decided to go out for dinner with Mike's parents to a quiet restaurant. We knew that if I nursed Hannah in the car before we went inside, she would sleep through the whole meal—and we could enjoy dinner and conversation with other adults.

The plan worked well. I nursed her; she fell asleep. We tucked her into the infant carrier and went into the restaurant for a quiet, relaxing dinner. We had a wonderful time eating and talking, talking and eating, and laughing a lot.

Throughout the meal, Hannah never made a sound. Never budged. Never cried or even whimpered. And when it was time to go home, we stood up and headed out. We had gotten about ten steps from the table when Mike and I both stopped in our tracks, stared at each other, and gasped.

We had forgotten Hannah.

She was still sleeping soundly in her infant carrier right next to our dinner table. Mike tried to act like everything was normal as he grabbed our most precious cargo. We left the restaurant in silence, but as soon as I got to the car, I burst into tears. I couldn't believe I almost forgot to bring my baby home! Mike lovingly reassured me that we would have remembered her...eventually. Several minutes later, we were chuckling at our inept parenting.

Thank God we got only ten feet away. And thank God for grace.

As our second, third, and fourth babies made their appearances and we were thrown again and again into baby mode, we learned to adapt. Eventually we just bundled up our little ones and headed out like cowboys on adventures—except ours were mostly by minivan.

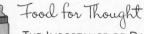 Food for Thought

THE IMPORTANCE OF DAD IN A BABY'S LIFE

Premature infants whose fathers spent more time playing with them had better mental outcomes at age three.

Children whose fathers were actively involved with them during the first eight weeks of life managed stress better as school-agers.

Children form attachments to fathers as well as mothers during months seven to thirteen.

Sons of nurturing fathers are more likely to model and internalize their modes of thinking and problem solving.

A close and warm relationship with Dad fosters a daughter's sense of competence, especially in math skills, and a secure sense of femininity.[2]

Over time we acquired every imaginable piece of baby equipment. I toted Sydney around in a sling carrier to cheer on the Bulldogs football team when Mike was coaching. We pulled her in a red wagon around the county fair. Colin loved to be carted in a backpack carrier; he must have felt like king of the world up there, because he was always content. Riley was a January baby—she spent her first spring snuggled under a nursing bib, eating away as I sat in a folding chair and cheered on the Bulldogs baseball team, which Mike was also coaching. I kept one eye on my nursing baby and the other on my three kids playing nearby. *Chomp, chomp.* "Sydney, stay near Mommy!" *Nibble, nibble.* "Let's go, Bulldogs!" *Suck, suck.* "Colin, don't put that rock in your mouth!" *Switch sides, do the tango. Burp baby, and do the two-step. Easy as pie.*

It Takes Two

It takes two grown-ups to raise a baby—a mom and a dad. Each brings unique parenting skills to a child's life, and they complement each other. The tricky issue is that moms and dads don't always parent, nurture, and care for their baby in the same way, and sometimes it is difficult for many moms to let go of their way and let Dad do things his way.

The great thing is that many dads are getting more involved today in their child's upbringing. This isn't just wonderful for all the moms who need the help; it's also a gift to all the babies who get to bond with Dad at an earlier age.

Mike was pretty comfortable with all of our babies. But then, he didn't have a choice. Throughout their early years I taught college two evenings a week, and during those evenings when I was gone, he became Mr. Mom.

But Mike didn't do things my way; he did things his way. And as different as those two ways were, both were fine. For example, I used to mix their rice cereal with some baby food to make it taste sweeter; Mike did it with formula. I used to bathe them every night; Mike only bathed them when they were dirty. I put their cutest, newest sleepers on them before bed; Mike put them in their oldest, hand-me-down, garage-sale pj's—anything with a tractor, a deer, or a football on them. It didn't matter if the feet were punching through or the knees had holes. It didn't even matter if the baby being dressed was a girl or a boy!

Letting go wasn't something that came easily to me. But over the years I have learned to let him be their dad—his way.

Now, I have to admit that I cringe when I come home after being gone and find all the kids dressed in tattered old mismatched barn clothes. Red stripes with purple plaid pants. Usually they have been playing outside for hours, their hair is unbrushed, and their faces and shoes are muddy. But, they all have smiles on their muddy little faces, and I know they had fun with Dad.

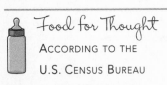

Food for Thought
ACCORDING TO THE U.S. CENSUS BUREAU

There are 189,000 stay-at-home dads and 11,000,000 stay-at-home moms in the United States.

The number of stay-at-home moms rose 13 percent between 1994 and 2002.

The number of stay-at-home dads increased by 18 percent from 1994 to 2002.[3]

All in all, we moms need to give our husbands a break. Give your husband a great big GET OUT OF TROUBLE FREE card. Don't critique his fathering. Let him play rough and wrestle on the floor. Let the kids go for pretend horse rides on his back and survive on Ritz crackers, cheese slices, and Juicy Juice.

Let your husband be the dad he already is.

FAITH ON FIRE

Dear Lord,

It is so reassuring to know that just as I comfort my baby, You are there to comfort me. My love for my child is only a reflection

*of Your love for both of us. As I experience the ups and downs
of my baby's first year of life, I pray that You guide and lead
me, protect and comfort me. Help me let go of my fears and let
my husband be the dad You intended him to be. As we work
together to raise this child, remind us to always seek You for the
answers.*
In Jesus's name,
amen.

Shelter from the Storm

*I used to stress about all the small stuff. Like whether my
baby was dressed in the perfect pink lace dress for church
or whether I was feeding her just the right baby food.
Once my second baby came along, I learned to relax
and not worry so much about the little things.
That's when I started truly enjoying motherhood.*

—JULIA H.

*My husband gives the baby a bath every night, and it has been awesome!
It allows him time to bond with the baby and me time to escape.
I usually end up reading the newspaper or napping on the
couch during my "leave of absence."*

—KENDRA M.

*My husband loves to wrestle on the family room floor
with the kids. Me? I usually stand by and worry about
whose head will hit the corner of the coffee table.
But I'm learning to let him be dad.*

—MALORIE B.

First-Aid Kit

Mom's BIG Questions Answered

★ **Breast or bottle.** With all the health benefits of breast-feeding for both baby and Mom, from boosting baby's immune system to reducing Mom's risk of breast cancer, it's a great idea to give breast-feeding a try. The colostrum secreted soon after birth is vital for baby, and you can always supplement with bottles.

★ **Crying it out.** You cannot spoil a newborn. Trust your instincts and soothe your crying baby on demand for at least the first few months. When the time is right, consult your pediatrician about a sleep system.

★ **Pacifier.** Not a big deal. Pacifier and thumbsucking will not impact your child's teeth until his permanent adult teeth are in. Talk to your pediatrician about the right time to wean your baby off the pacifier.

★ **Crib.** Spend your money on a nice crib and don't spend a lot on a new bassinet. Babies outgrow bassinets so quickly; if you use one at all, try to find a used one.

★ **Changing table.** Not necessary. I found that most of the time I changed my baby on a blanket on the floor. It was just easier. But if you get the whole nursery furniture set and it comes with it, you can use it for storage or use it as a laundry sorting table when you're no longer doing diapers.

★ **Disposable diapers.** Stock up early on size one and two when they are on sale. Most babies outgrow the newborn size pretty fast. Also, keep in mind that you can exchange unopened bags of diapers for the next size you need.

★ **Cloth diapers.** If you decide to use cloth diapers, there are many kinds available. Some, called all-in-ones (AIO), have the plastic

pants built in; others will need a separate plastic outer. Pick the
kind that works best for you.

★ **Baby wipes.** A must-have. If you want to make your own homemade baby wipes to save money, you can search online for a
recipe.

★ **Baby monitor.** A must-have, especially for first-time moms. And
when your kids get older, you can use it to check on them as well.

★ **Diaper disposal system.** Many moms love these, but not me. I
never took the time to drop, twist, and turn—too complicated.
However, now there are systems on the market that are easy to
use, a simple front to back turn, and can accommodate regular tall
kitchen garbage bags.

★ **Bouncy seat.** I felt it was a waste of money, but some moms swear
by them—especially if they include a vibrating feature. Try to find
a used one or request it as a shower gift.

★ **Swing.** In my experience, this is worth its weight in gold! Invest in
the best and keep plenty of batteries on hand! Or invest in
rechargeable batteries.

★ **Playpen.** Get the fold-up, travel-friendly kind. You will use this
until your baby is two or three. It's a great place for implementing
time-out or keeping toddlers safe while you take a shower, cook
supper, or do laundry.

★ **Car seat.** According to the American Academy of Pediatrics, children should face the rear of the vehicle until they are at least one
year old and weigh at least twenty pounds. You can use an infant
carrier car seat or convertible seat until the baby outgrows it by
weight, positioned semireclined and rear facing, until one year of
age and at least twenty pounds.[4]

S.O.S.
(Spiritual Opportunity to Savor)

The next day Jesus decided to leave for Galilee. Finding Philip, he said to him, "Follow me."

Philip, like Andrew and Peter, was from the town of Bethsaida. Philip found Nathanael and told him, "We have found the one Moses wrote about in the Law, and about whom the prophets also wrote—Jesus of Nazareth, the son of Joseph."

"Nazareth! Can anything good come from there?" Nathanael asked.

"Come and see," said Philip.

When Jesus saw Nathanael approaching, he said of him, "Here is a true Israelite, in whom there is nothing false."

"How do you know me?" Nathanael asked.

Jesus answered, "I saw you while you were still under the fig tree before Philip called you."

Then Nathanael declared, "Rabbi, you are the Son of God; you are the King of Israel."

Jesus said, "You believe because I told you I saw you under the fig tree. You shall see greater things than that."

JOHN 1:43–50

 Take Heart, Rookie Mom

Motherhood is like boot camp for life. We learn patience, kindness, sacrificial giving, and love. Boy, do we learn about love during our mothering years.

Not the easy kind of love, either, with roses, candy, and flowers.

Nope—this kind of love is far beyond what we can imagine. It's the kind of love that sees you through six months of sleepless nights and more stress and frustration than you ever imagined surviving.

I have been a mom now for a dozen years, so I guess I seem like a veteran to some. However, I have friends with teenagers and even adult children and grandchildren, and to them I seem like the rookie mom still making rookie mistakes.

Personally, I think I fall somewhere in between. When my first baby was born, I was most definitely a rookie mom. Aren't we blessed that God calls rookies into His ministry? Motherhood is the most important ministry you will ever have.

Jesus called Philip and Nathanael, and they were rookies. They had no idea what they were getting into when they felt the calling to follow Jesus. Likewise, we have no idea what we're getting into when we first become moms.

I struggle each day to meet my kids' needs and still reserve some energy and emotion for my own needs and my husband's needs. That struggle is most difficult when you have a baby in your arms.

But rest assured that you are the perfect mom for your baby. God said so the moment your baby came into your life, and He will be there with you each step of the way. He likes calling rookies into His ministry. So, Rookie Mom, lean on Him and await the "greater things" God has in store for your life.

Study Questions

1. Do you feel like a rookie mom? a veteran mom? someone in between?
2. What mom fears do you have?

3. What parts of motherhood are you more confident in? What do you already do well?

4. How is God working in your life to help you be the mom He desires you to be?

5. Is there an older mom who can be your mentor mom? Pray about this and ask her if she is willing to advise you in your mothering skills. And be willing to listen.

Blazing New Trails

Getting to Know Your Husband All Over Again

Water from the Word
*Love is patient, love is kind. It does not envy, it does not boast,
it is not proud. It is not rude, it is not self-seeking, it is not
easily angered, it keeps no record of wrongs.*
1 CORINTHIANS 13:4–5

When I first met Mike in college, I never imagined how our life would be. All I knew was that he smiled at me in Business Statistics class and had the cutest dimples and the sweetest eyes I had ever seen. Aah, my heart melted right from the start. I didn't think much past the next weekend and trying to get him to ask me out, let alone years down the road and the family we might have. I also never imagined how much sports would become a part of my life.

When I met Mike, he was playing football for Baldwin-Wallace College—defensive tackle, to be precise. And in the blink of an eye, I was spending every autumn Saturday afternoon sitting in the bleachers cheering on the Yellow Jackets and hoping Mike didn't get injured by some huge offensive lineman.

Another thing happened our first autumn together. I fell in love with

Mike. I also soon discovered that Friday nights before football games, Mike got pretty stressed out and usually would pick a fight with me over nothing at all. It didn't take long to realize that we handled our emotions differently. Once I recognized that, life with Mike was a whole lot better.

But getting to know each other doesn't end when you stop dating and get married. In fact, as the years go by, it typically grows *more* complex as life hands you one challenge after another.

It has been more than eighteen years since I met Mike, and I am still learning how to communicate, live with, and love him best. As frustrating as those Friday nights were in college, I have felt the same way at times in my marriage. Mike and I were simply made differently, both as men and women and as unique individuals created by God. We react and communicate in very different ways and on very different levels, and it is a challenge at times to see each other's perspective. For example, when things go wrong, I want to talk about it and Mike wants to act. I want to analyze my bad day; he wants to fix it for me.

Communication in marriage is difficult even *before* you add a baby to the mix. Along with that precious little baby comes exhaustion, frustration, stress, and, if you're not careful, anger and resentment.

Food for Thought

MEN COMMUNICATE DIFFERENTLY THAN WOMEN

Men talk less. On average, they say about half as many words as women do in the course of a day.[1]

Men are bottom-line oriented. In order to communicate more effectively with them, try getting directly to the point.

Men want specifics, not all the details. Don't expect your husband to converse with you in the same way your girlfriends do. Try being more direct and less detailed with him.

What Do Men Care About?

Is it sports? sex? career?

The answer, of course, is all or some of the above. You can also add "providing for their family," "loving their wife," and "fathering their children." But most of all, "following Christ and leading their family in their faith."

Boy, that's a huge load to carry, isn't it?

Believe it or not, men are not as black and white as we might think. They are as complex as women; they just tend to hide it deep inside and not open up as easily as we do.

In her book *For Women Only,* author Shaunti Feldhahn conducted extensive research into the inner lives of men. She discovered seven basic truths that we, as wives, need to know about our husbands:

What You Need to Know About Men by Shaunti Feldhahn[2]

- **Men need respect.** Men would rather feel unloved than inadequate and disrespected.
- **Men are insecure.** Despite their "in control" exterior, men often feel like impostors and are insecure that their inadequacies will be discovered.
- **Men are providers.** Even if you personally made enough income to support the family's lifestyle, it would make no difference to the mental burden he feels to provide.
- **Men want more sex.** Your sexual desire for your husband profoundly affects his sense of well-being and confidence in all areas of life.
- **Men are visual.** Even happily married men struggle with being pulled toward live and recollected images of other women.

- **Men are unromantic clods.** Actually, most men enjoy romance (sometimes in different ways) and want to be romantic—but hesitate because they doubt they can succeed.
- **Men care about appearance.** You don't need to be a size 4, but your man needs to see you making the effort to take care of yourself.

As wives, we can better love, understand, and communicate with our husbands during the parenting years if we take the time to understand where they are coming from. Understanding your husband will also open the door for better teamwork as you parent your new baby together.

So no more sitting on the sidelines, ladies. It's time to get in the game, and love and respect your husband just as he is!

Men need respect

When I became pregnant with Hannah, Mike and I decided that I would quit my full-time job in marketing to be a stay-at-home mom. I was ready to quit; it was the right time for me.

However, I also wanted to stay active in my career. Once Hannah was born, I was able to stay at home during the day and teach an hour-long college class on Tuesday and Thursday evenings at the local university. My schedule went something like this: I would nurse Hannah at 5 p.m., walk out the door at 5:30, and teach class from 6:00 to 7:15, hoping and praying that my breasts didn't leak in the middle of the lecture. At the end of class, I would rush home to nurse Hannah again.

The first week I went back to teaching, I arrived home on those evenings to find Mike walking laps around the house, bouncing a crying, hungry Hannah in his arms. Then Mike suggested that I pump a few ounces beforehand or that he give her formula on those two evenings while I was gone.

My first thought was, *Are you kidding? She needs* me, *not some bottle!* But instead of writing off Mike's suggestion, I took a deep breath and agreed that it might be a good idea. I allowed him to make that decision; I respected his input.

In the end, he was right—we were able to combine breast-feeding and bottle-feeding. I could be gone two evenings a week without feeling panicked about getting home in time to nurse Hannah, and Mike was able to feed her and meet her needs in my absence.

The most important lesson I learned, however, wasn't about deciding to combine breast-feeding with bottle-feeding. Rather, it was how critical it is that I respect Mike's ability to father our baby. My listening to his opinion made him feel valued as a father, and it improved our marriage.

With the arrival of your firstborn, you probably feel the weight of the world on your shoulders. After all, *you're* the mom. You carried that baby in your belly for nine months. You spend a great deal of time with your baby. And if you're breast-feeding, you're even the source of your baby's nourishment. It's natural that you feel like the baby expert in your marriage. Perhaps at times you even put down your husband's parenting skills. He doesn't know how to feed the baby; he diapers all wrong; he is unable to soothe your baby's crying.

Food for Thought

Marriage counselors recommend that spouses spend at least twenty seconds kissing each other every day.[3]

Have you met today's minimum requirement? If not, pucker up!

But your husband is doing things right; it's just different from the way you are doing them. It's kind of a learn-as-you-go life lesson, and you need to allow him the time and room to find his way. You also need to respect him as the father of your baby. The respect you give in this area of his life will impact your marriage in many other ways for years to come.

Men are insecure

The other day I took the kids to see the movie *Shrek the Third*. After spending two hours in the theater, I left with a much greater understanding of and appreciation for my husband.

In the movie, Prince Charming and the Fairy Godmother are actually the bad guys, and Shrek—the big, ugly ogre—is the good guy, the hero, the love of Fiona's life. But as accomplished and beloved as Shrek is, he is also very insecure about who he is, how he looks, and impending fatherhood.

Who would have figured *that*?

Now, Mike is not an ogre (just wanted to clarify that). But like Shrek, he is the hero of our family. I think of him as big and strong, the one who takes care of us, the go-to guy in my life. That's a lot of pressure for one person.

Men are insecure about themselves just like we are. When they become fathers, those insecurities multiply. They may feel unprepared to lead their children by example, whether they had the best dad in the world or the worst.

One thing you can do is to reassure your husband. Tell him what a wonderful father he is and what a great job he's doing. Words are powerful, and something as simple as "Honey, thank you for taking the baby to the park yesterday. She has so much fun with you" can go a long way toward encouraging and empowering your husband to be more confident in his fathering. Trust that he is able to care for the baby when you can't be there. That one-on-one time between father and baby is crucial for their bonding and for your husband's confidence in his fathering.

Most important, believe in your husband. After all, you picked him to father your children. Trust him to be the dad God created him to be.

Men are providers

Before Mike and I had kids, I helped provide financially by working full-time as a marketing manager. Now I write and teach college part-time and still bring in a little bit of money, but Mike is the main financial provider for our family.

Men are called to provide for their families, and they take pride in doing so. With that calling, however, comes the stress of responsibility. I have watched friends and family struggle through tough financial times, and I have observed how devastating it can be to a man's confidence when he is unable to provide for his family.

Your husband feels the need to provide for you even if you work outside the home before and after you have children. Now that he is responsible for children, the pressure is really on. I will always remember the day Mike finally received his tenure at work, meaning that he had job security. He was so joyful. Of course, as a high-school teacher, he'll never make a fortune. But to him it was more important to have the security of that income than to make a million bucks.

Men are created by God to be providers. We need to encourage them, support them in that provision, and allow them to provide for us. Even if you work outside the home, even if you earn more than your husband does, look to him and respect him as the provider, and watch the blessings flow.

Men want more sex

Sex is a big deal in marriage. Think about it: Would you have married your husband if you weren't physically attracted to him? And if you weren't attracted to him, would you have desired to make a baby together?

When you think about it, it's pretty ironic that in order to have a baby you have to have sex, but once you have the baby, the sex often disappears! In her book *We Should Do This More Often,* author Lorilee

Craker discusses the fact that 87 percent of moms said that they didn't have sex with their husbands as often as they had before becoming a mom, while 33 percent said that their love life took a "major nose-dive" after having a baby.[4]

There's an old story about a husband who accompanies his wife to her six-week checkup. He boldly asks the doctor if it's okay to have sex now, and the doctor gives him the green light; the wife rolls her eyes. So they go home. He gently places the baby in the battery-operated swing, belts him in tightly, and takes his wife's hand. "Let's go, honey!" he says. "I read the directions, and this swing can go for at least thirty minutes!"

(Of course, this story serves as a great reason *not* to take your husband to your six-week ob-gyn checkup!)

Your man needs you; he wants you. And no, he doesn't just see you as the mother of his child. He still sees you as the hot chick who stole his heart and sparked his libido before you had kids.

Make sex a priority in your marriage. If you haven't quite worked up the enthusiasm to enjoy sex yet, close your eyes and enjoy it for your husband's sake. Believe it or not, your love life will soon be back on track. A man sees love in sex and feels loved when you share your body with him. Don't underestimate that power.

Bottom line: Don't let go of the intimacy you and your husband both desire and need.

Men are visual

Mike grew up on a two-hundred-acre farm, much of it woods. One Christmas while we were dating, I helped him gather evergreen swags in the woods for his mom to decorate her porch with. A day later, my face and neck swelled up with a rash that made me look like a circus sideshow. It itched like crazy. Apparently, I was allergic to pine sap.

I made an appointment with a dermatologist, and Mike, caring boyfriend that he was, went along with me. In walked the doctor, tall and thin, with long blond hair and blue eyes. She was beautiful; in fact, she looked more like a *Vogue* model than a dermatologist. And there I was, not looking my best (to say the least).

As she entered the exam room, I quickly glanced over at Mike and saw his jaw about drop to the ground. When he caught my eye, I gave him a *look* through my swollen cheeks, a look that he knew meant "tuck your eyes back into your head and stop gawking."

Men are very visual. They are constantly pulled toward visual images of beautiful women, either in person or in the card file of memories stored in their head. That doctor's visit happened almost eighteen years ago, and to this day we still laugh and joke about it, and I remind Mike to keep his eyes on me.

Girlfriends, it is very easy to let yourself go. I know I have done that over the years. Having four babies can do a real number on your body, and it is difficult to get back on track physically. You don't have to be a size 4. You don't have to be a *Vogue* model. You don't have to be perfect. But you do need to take care of yourself physically and be the best you can be.

Start exercising, but keep it simple. Walk around the block with the baby in the stroller. Join an exercise class at the local YMCA where they offer free baby-sitting. Drink lots of water, eat healthy foods, and do your best to stay in shape. Get a few girlfriends together to work toward meeting health goals. In the long run you will be healthier, and your husband's jaw will drop when he sees you walk up the driveway. Isn't that worth it?

By the way, the gorgeous doctor gave me a shot that cured my allergic reaction, and soon enough I was back to my old self again, wooing Mike with my own brown eyes.

 Food for Thought

TEN KEYS TO A SUCCESSFUL MARRIAGE

Key 1. Be committed

…to your faith in Christ, your husband, and your marriage.

Key 2. Be sexually intimate

…on a regular basis, meeting each other's needs.

Key 3. Be respectful

…of each other's careers, dreams, and goals.

Key 4. Be romantic

…even when you don't feel romantic.

Key 5. Be a team

…as you make decisions, never disagreeing in front of the children.

Key 6. Be willing to say, "I'm sorry"

…when you make a mistake, and even sometimes when you don't.

Key 7. Be willing to forgive

…whenever your husband earnestly apologizes.

Key 8. Be full of praise

…for your husband, complimenting him and praising him to others.

Key 9. Spend time together

…on a regular basis, with *and* without your children around.

Key 10. Be loving

…toward your husband. Hold his hand or kiss him gently—just because.[6]

Men are unromantic clods

Most men enjoy romance, but they're afraid of getting it wrong. When Mike and I were in college and dating, we would meet for lunch at the dining hall and then walk across the quad to class. Mike would reach to carry my books for me, and I would inevitably grab them back from him. I didn't see his carrying my books as a romantic gesture; I saw it as intrusive. But Mike viewed it as chivalrous. He also opened doors for me and paid for all our dates. He treated me like a princess. Yet somehow my view of romance was different from his. I wanted him to get it right, which meant my way.

When did we women make the romance rules so complicated? and so secretive?

When you bring that baby home from the hospital, the last thing on your mind is romance. But once you have settled in at home with your new baby, don't let too much time go by without it.

Romance does not have to be expensive or complicated. It can be as simple as leaving a love note for your husband on the kitchen table, or putting the baby down to bed and having a candlelit dinner at home.

And be sure to let your husband know what you think is romantic. Tell him. Be straight about it. He is not a mind reader, after all. Be specific about what is romantic to you and then watch as he romances you all over again.

Now I let Mike carry things for me. I love it when he opens the door for me. I also tell him what I like and pay attention to what he likes in the romance department. It's really more about love than sex—taking the time to do and say the things that your spouse likes. Don't make your husband feel like he is getting it wrong. Help him get it right!

Men care about appearance

The first few months of motherhood are kind of a blur for me. I was only getting an hour or two of consecutive sleep at night, so getting dressed in nice khakis and curling my hair did not make my list of priorities.

But when Hannah was only a week old, my in-laws invited Mike, Hannah, and me out to dinner. I took the time to shower, do my hair and makeup, and dress in a going-out-to-dinner outfit, pumps and all. I still remember the look on Mike's face when I came downstairs. It was as if he were seeing me for the first time. It was nice to get *that* look again.

Men see things differently than women do, and what they see is important to them. They care about how we look. Like it or not, appearance matters. They fell in love with us inside and out, and though the inside is vitally more important in the scheme of things, the outside shouldn't be overlooked either.

Spending the first year of motherhood in your flannel pajamas with unwashed, messy hair and no makeup may not be honoring to your husband or yourself. And it certainly doesn't build your confidence.

Now ladies, I'm *not* saying that you shouldn't give yourself a break. During those first few months following birth, it's tough enough to worry about meeting all the baby's needs—let alone care about your appearance. But you must realize that your baby is not the king of the house and that the best gift you can give your baby is to have a strong, intimate relationship with his father. Part of that is caring enough to look good for your husband.

Then, when you get *that* look from your sweetheart, all your efforts will be worth it!

Accept Him as He Is

When I married a high-school teacher and coach, I quickly discovered that fall meant football and spring meant baseball.

I still go to almost all of Mike's games. Not because I enjoy running after four kids, sitting in cold bleachers, or waving a pompom, but because I love Mike just as he is. And he is a coach.

Part of the way I show Mike unconditional love is by not trying to change him into something he isn't. After all, Mike accepts *me*, quirks and all (like writing a book in which I discuss our marriage for the world to see). I also talk way too much, stay up too late at night to watch mindless television, and leave the toothpaste cap untwisted.

Marriage is a fantastic state of mind, a lifelong commitment that often introduces new life in the blessed form of children. But if you are not careful, those very same children can be your marriage's undoing.

So talk to your husband. Listen to him. Romance and respect him. Give yourself to him even when you aren't sure you can give any more. Then be ready to unwrap one of God's greatest gifts: a loving husband!

Faith on Fire

Dear Lord,
As we venture out on this new path of parenting, help us remember that we are husband and wife first. As tiring as parenting is, help us make time for each other and to prioritize our marriage. As we look for pockets of time, little spots for love, help us cherish and make more of them for each other. Remind us that our shared commitment to our marriage is the greatest gift we can give our children. In Jesus's name,
amen.

Shelter from the Storm

Ethan is one year old, and I have found that my husband and I do things differently with him. When I tuck Ethan into bed,

I read a book to him, rock him, and sing to him. I take my time
and enjoy the process. When my husband does the bedtime routine
and comes back downstairs in five minutes, I ask, "Did you even
read him a book?" He does, just faster. Men are so goal-oriented,
and his goal is getting Ethan to bed.

—MARY BETH D.

I really miss eating meals with my husband, the spontaneity
of going out and doing stuff together at the drop of a hat,
going to bed together and having conversations as we drift off to sleep.
And, at this point, I miss the sex.

—ALLISON L.

I'm a grandma now, but I still remember my first visit to the
doctor with my newborn twins. After he examined the twins and
proclaimed they were thriving, he sat back and asked if I was
making time for Dad. Who? Was he crazy? I had two babies that
kept me busy every minute of the day and a good part of the night.
When was I supposed to sleep, let alone take care of my husband?

—KAREN R.

As my focus shifted from my husband to my baby daughter,
I occasionally noticed a faraway look in his eyes that
conveyed a combination of missing me and mild envy.

—BRENDA N.

Having a son gave me a window into how my husband used to be as
a boy. My son even walks like him. So, basically having a child brought
another dimension into our marriage in the way I perceive my husband.

—SUSAN T.

*Now that we have our son, we have a really strong reason
to go out of our way to build our marriage because the best gift
we can give him is a mom and dad who love each other.*

—MELANIE M.

*I saw my husband in a different light after our baby was born.
I fell in love with him all over again.*

—LYNETTE M.

FIRST-AID KIT

☆ **Tag-team approach.** Give up the idea of caring for your baby 50-
50 with your husband, especially if you are a stay-at-home-mom.
You are the mom, and as much as Dad helps, most of the baby
stuff still falls to you. But after dinner, try the tag-team approach.
For instance, have him bathe the baby while you clean the high
chair.

☆ **Talk and talk.** Once the baby is in bed and you both crawl under
the covers for much-needed sleep, take a few minutes to talk to
each other about your day. Even five minutes can be beneficial to
your marriage.

☆ **Date night.** Go out on a date once a month while Grandma
baby-sits—it's a great way to reconnect. If money is tight, try taking a baby-free walk around the block or a trip to the coffee shop.

☆ **Sex.** Don't stress about sex. You will eventually feel turned on again.
Until then, try faking it for a while. Before you know it, you'll be
in the mood naturally, and you might even be the initiator!

☆ **Date at home.** Don't underestimate the fun you can have right at
home. Tuck the baby in bed, rent a romantic movie, pop some
popcorn, and snuggle up on the couch together. Of course, if you

both fall asleep in the middle of the movie, no one will know how it ended. But you will end up spending wonderful time with your spouse.

☆ **Value him.** Show your husband how much you appreciate the help you get from him. Pay him lots of compliments; praise and thank him for his contributions. You will be amazed by how much more help you get when you encourage an active role in his child's life.

☆ **Make time.** Prioritize quality time with your husband in *and* out of the bedroom. Talk to him without nagging. Ask him about his day. Seek his advice. Listen to his heart. Sure, it takes effort. But the best gift you can give your baby is a healthy, loving marriage.

S.O.S.
(Spiritual Opportunity to Savor)

How beautiful your sandaled feet,
  O prince's daughter!
Your graceful legs are like jewels,
  the work of a craftsman's hands.
Your navel is a rounded goblet
  that never lacks blended wine.
Your waist is a mound of wheat
  encircled by lilies.
Your breasts are like two fawns,
  twins of a gazelle.
Your neck is like an ivory tower.
Your eyes are the pools of Heshbon
  by the gate of Bath Rabbim.

Your nose is like the tower of Lebanon
  looking toward Damascus.
Your head crowns you like Mount Carmel.
  Your hair is like royal tapestry;
  the king is held captive by its tresses.
How beautiful you are and how pleasing,
  O love, with your delights!
Your stature is like that of the palm,
  and your breasts like clusters of fruit.
I said, "I will climb the palm tree;
  I will take hold of its fruit."
May your breasts be like the clusters of the vine,
  the fragrance of your breath like apples,
and your mouth like the best wine.

SONG OF SOLOMON 7:1–9

 Love in Many Forms

When I was in high school, I thought I was in love. His name was Sean, and he was tall with blue eyes and a tender heart. But as the weeks turned into months and then years, our dating relationship became more about how I could meet his needs, not a give-and-take, sacrificial kind of love. I learned the hard way that love is complex and that I needed to grow up and grow in my faith before I was ready for marriage.

Through that failed relationship, I learned a lot about myself and what I *didn't* want in a husband. I am convinced that it helped prepare my heart and soul not only to seek true love but also to seek and accept the ultimate love of Christ as well.

By the time I met Mike, I knew what I was looking for in love. However, I was surprised to find even more than I had hoped for. Mike introduced me to the Christ of his heart, and within a year, I had accepted Christ as my Savior as well.

Many biblical scholars talk about three kinds of love. I think each is of vital importance to a solid, godly marriage.

First is *phileo* love, the tender affection you feel toward your husband. Most of our friendships are built on *phileo* love. It is the love that draws you toward another person and helps you build a friendship with him or her.

Next is *eros* love. *Eros* love is what attracts you to your husband. It is the hubba-hubba feeling you get when he looks at you and your knees grow weak. It is the sexual desire you feel for him. And just as God's plan calls for, it is in marriage that two become one flesh.

Finally is *agape* love. Agape love is the highest form of love. It is unconditional, always forgiving, always accepting. It lasts when all other forms of love call it quits. *Agape* love comes from God and was exemplified in its purest form when Jesus took on our sin and died for us on the cross.

Marriage is a mosaic of these three kinds of love. It may begin with *phileo,* when we first form a friendship during the dating years. It soon moves toward *eros,* as we desire to be physically closer to our mate. And through marriage, we fulfill the *agape* form of love in a committed relationship.

When you bring that precious baby home from the hospital and desire sleep more than you desire your husband, it is very easy to fall into the *phileo* form of love and stay there for too long. But God wants all three forms of love in our marriages. As difficult as it may be to realize, you *are* the desire of your husband's heart and body. As the Song of Songs says, you are "beautiful" and "pleasing" to your husband.

During these mommy years, don't forget that you were a wife first and will be a wife long after your kids leave for college. Build that intimacy with your husband and say yes in the bedroom. Just watch how God blesses your marriage.

Study Questions

1. How many times this week have you said no to your husband's desire for intimacy?
2. When was the last time you had a heart-to-heart talk with your husband about your marriage?
3. How can you make time for each other on a regular basis?
4. Write down three things you can do to make your husband feel special. Do them this week.

Covering New Ground

The Unique Gift of Your Baby

Water from the Word
And even the very hairs of your head are
all numbered. So don't be afraid;
you are worth more than many sparrows.
MATTHEW 10:30–31

Even before I became a mom, I knew exactly what my baby would look like: She would have dark brown hair, dark brown eyes, and deep dimples—a cookie-cutter version of Mike and me.

Boy, was I surprised by Hannah's bright blue eyes and peach-fuzz hair! In fact, if I hadn't given birth to her, I might have questioned whether she was my baby at all. I couldn't believe it when Hannah's hair stayed light and her eyes stayed blue, either.

I asked my pediatrician about the probability of our having a blue-eyed baby. He said that blue eyes are recessive, which means Mike and I must both carry that trait. Between us, we had only a 25 percent chance of having a blue-eyed child. Well, guess what? We ended up with *four* blue-eyed children! (We sure beat the odds...maybe we should play the lottery.) Hannah, Colin, and Riley all have very light brown hair, and only Sydney has our thick, dark brown hair. Her eyes are so light blue they seem to glow in the dark.

Not only did I picture my kids looking just like me, I also pictured them acting just like one another. But God had other plans. My children not only have their own looks; they each have their own personality, as unique as I ever imagined, and their own love language.

 Food for Thought

THE FIVE LOVE LANGUAGES OF CHILDREN

1. **Physical Touch**

Spend time hugging and snuggling with your child, touching him when you talk to him, rubbing his back before bed, and holding his hand in yours.

2. **Words of Affirmation**

Tell your child you love her, how proud you are of her.

3. **Quality Time**

Make sure to spend one-on-one time with your child daily and give him your full attention.

4. **Gifts**

Give your child lots of little gifts that reflect your love for her.

5. **Acts of Service**

Do special things for your child, like making his bed or helping him with a project.[1]

The Seasons of Life

When my first baby was born, I wanted to do everything right. I read all the books, followed the experts' advice, and bought every piece of recommended equipment. I wore myself out trying to be a perfect mother.

But I have evolved over the years into a much more comfortable mom. I survived four first years of motherhood with four very unique kids, none of whom is exactly like me. (That would be way too easy!)

I've discovered that my job as their mom isn't to change who they are. Instead, my responsibility is to love and accept them for who they are, and help them grow up to become men and women of character who love Christ.

Even now, with over a decade of mothering under my belt, I'm still learning about my four children in each new stage of development. I've discovered that they are a lot like the four seasons we experience here in the Midwest: Hannah is snuggling under an old quilt next to a fireplace in the wintertime, Sydney is planting bright pink impatiens in the spring, Colin is running barefoot through the sprinkler in the summer, and Riley is jumping into a pile of crisp autumn leaves in the fall. And also like the changing seasons, each of my children brings a new and pleasant sense of joy, pride, and uniqueness to my life.

My winter child

From the moment Hannah was born, she was a snuggler. Like a blazing fire on a cold winter's night, she warms me with her tender heart and teaches me daily about compassion and understanding.

As a newborn, Hannah loved it best when we held her close. She relaxed when she felt our touches, strokes, and hugs. As I've mentioned, she was never a good sleeper as a baby, keeping us up more nights than I care to remember.

Hannah was also a fast learner, walking at nine months, repeating our words at one year, and memorizing *Goodnight Moon* at just under two, when her little sister, Sydney, was born.

Today, at twelve years old, Hannah is still not a great sleeper. We call her the Comeback Kid, because no matter when we tuck her into bed, she always finds a reason to make her way downstairs to see us again. She is also an avid reader, an honor student, and an athlete, all traits I can now trace back with 20/20 hindsight to her baby years.

My spring child

Sydney entered this world the same way she lives in it today—full of serenity and beauty. (I slept through her labor, thanks to an amazing epidural!) Like a bright red tulip bursting through the spring soil, Sydney brings great joy into our lives and always reminds me to embrace life with a smile.

Sydney was born with a full head of dark hair—so much, in fact, that it resembled a toupee! One of my most embarrassing "mom moments" happened the day after Sydney was born. I took a leisurely walk to the hospital nursery to get Sydney because it was time to nurse her, and as I approached the glass window, I saw that there were only two babies in the nursery: one little boy and one adorable little Asian baby girl.

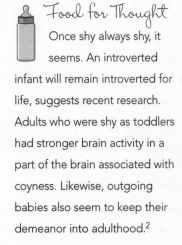

Food for Thought

Once shy always shy, it seems. An introverted infant will remain introverted for life, suggests recent research. Adults who were shy as toddlers had stronger brain activity in a part of the brain associated with coyness. Likewise, outgoing babies also seem to keep their demeanor into adulthood.[2]

I started to panic. *Where is Sydney? Why isn't she in the nursery? Did someone take her?*

I picked up my pace, practically sprinting to the nursery window. Suddenly I realized that the little Asian girl *was* Sydney. My hyperventilating stopped, and I looked around to see if anyone had witnessed my antics.

Nope. The coast was clear. *Whew.*

Sydney's hair was so thick and black, and her face had been squished so much during her birth (because she weighed as much as a Volkswagen Beetle and had a head the size of a watermelon), that she looked slightly Asian—from a distance. Can I also blame my error on a long labor that probably blurred my vision or destroyed my brain cells?

From the moment we brought her home, Sydney was a great sleeper. In fact, on our first night home from the hospital, I tucked her in the crib and then woke with a start four hours later because she hadn't made a peep. I ran into the nursery to find her sound asleep, content as could be—a far cry from Hannah's feed-me-every-hour and walk-me-around-the-house first sleepless night home.

That was my first eye-opening experience that my kids weren't carbon copies of one another, and that they didn't come with instruction manuals.

As a baby, Sydney did not like to be held. She preferred to lie on a blanket on the floor so she could kick her feet freely. She was quiet and very easygoing. Today, at ten years old, Sydney is still Miss Independent, preferring to play Barbies or My Little Ponies all by herself in her bedroom. She has to be coaxed to sit on my lap and snuggle on the couch. She has become quite a good reader, is an honor student, enjoys basketball, makes up the most amazing stories, and plays pretend like an Oscar-winning actress.

My summer child

Colin entered this world like a blast of fireworks on a hot summer night, and he continues to light up my life with his enthusiasm, energy, and love. My pregnancy with Colin was a roller coaster ride of ups and downs. Two weeks before his due date, my water broke at home, and he was born with a bang less than two hours later! (Yes, we made it to the hospital in time, and no, there was no time for the epidural to kick in.)

After having had two girls, I couldn't imagine having a boy. We were all sugar and spice and everything nice at our house! Right from the start, Colin was all frogs and snails and puppy dog tails. He was born with his feet moving at hyperspeed—he wanted to crawl and walk before he could even hold his head up straight.

As a baby, Colin was a pretty good sleeper but always an early riser. He was so active during the daytime that when his bedtime came around, I tucked him in and collapsed on the couch with a huge sigh. When he hit two years old, I stopped taking him to the grocery store, because I didn't have the strength to chase him up and down the aisles, and there was no way he would sit still in a shopping cart.

Food for Thought

During your baby's first year of life, his brain will grow in size from 400 grams to a whopping 1,000 grams. The first two years are critical for brain development. This is the period when babies' brains develop mental patterns that will dictate their behavior through adulthood.

Developing an emotional connection with your baby is much more important during the first two years of his life than pushing "baby genius" tapes or other forms of intellectual learning.

A well-nurtured sense of love and security has a much greater impact on his developing intellect in the long run. So relax, and just play with your baby![3]

Today, at eight years old, Colin is full of smiles, life, and joy. He loves people and attention, and he enjoys wrestling on the family room floor with his dad and hitting baseballs in the front yard. I don't think his feet have stopped moving yet.

He also has an amazing heart for people, loving and hugging everyone he meets. At church, during the worship service when we "share the peace" (shake hands with everyone near you and say "peace be with you"), Colin takes almost twenty minutes to walk around the entire sanctuary shaking hands with everybody he can reach. People look forward to his handshakes and hugs, and many have said that Colin will grow up to be either a pastor or a politician. (I'm rooting for pastor, just in case you were wondering.)

My autumn child

Riley was born with her own agenda. In fact, I was so uncomfortable during my pregnancy with her that I felt certain she had a Day Planner tucked away somewhere! She lives life a lot like an autumn leaf blowing in the wind, floating along on her own path, and I'm thankful to be along for the ride.

I truly thought Riley was going to be a boy because she was so active, kicking and punching me night and day. But God blessed us with an amazing little girl who has her own ideas and a mission to conquer the world.

As a newborn, Riley was my worst sleeper. She didn't like the bassinet, crib, swing, car seat, or floor; she wanted to sleep right on top of Mom, and she got her way for the first three months. I have a feeling Riley will get her way a lot in this life because she is such a determined, self-motivated little girl. Today, at five years old, her biggest phrases are "Me too" and "What about Riley?" She always wants to be in the mix of things, and she has always seemed older than her years. She longs to keep up with her big sisters and brother so badly that she jumps into everything headfirst without fear.

No Instruction Manual

Kids don't follow a simple path in life. There is no doctor, expert, or book out there that will adequately explain your unique child to you. I have yet to locate the instruction manual that comes with a baby! You just have to figure it out as you go, pray a lot, and hope for the best.

But we do have the best Teacher in the world. He even cares enough about us to number the hairs on our heads! The same God who created us will help you mother your children if you ask Him. Our children may not follow the rules by the book, but they were created by the One who wrote the Book, and that Book has all the answers you will ever need.

Food for Thought

THE EVOLUTION OF MOTHERHOOD

YOUR CLOTHES

First baby. You begin wearing maternity clothes as soon as your ob-gyn confirms your pregnancy.

Second baby. You wear your regular clothes for as long as possible.

Third baby. Your maternity clothes *are* your regular clothes.

PREPARING FOR THE BIRTH

First baby. You practice your breathing religiously.

Second baby. You don't bother practicing because you remember that last time, breathing didn't do a thing.

Third baby. You ask for an epidural in your eighth month.

THE LAYETTE

First baby. You prewash your newborn's clothes, color coordinate them, and fold them neatly in baby's little bureau.

Second baby. You check to make sure that the clothes are clean and discard only the ones with the darkest stains.

Third baby. Boys can wear pink, can't they?

ACTIVITIES

First baby. You take your infant to Baby Gymnastics, Baby Swing, and Baby Story Hour.

Second baby. You take your infant to Baby Gymnastics.

Third baby. You take your infant to the supermarket and the dry cleaner.

AT HOME

First baby. You spend a good bit of every day just gazing at the baby.

Second baby. You spend a bit of every day watching to be sure your older child isn't squeezing, poking, or hitting the baby.

Third baby. You spend a little bit of every day hiding from the children.[4]

FAITH ON FIRE

Dear Lord,
Thank You for knitting my precious little one together and
making him unique. I know that I sometimes expect my baby
to be a cookie-cutter version of me, and I might not under-
stand when he is not. Help me see the beauty of my baby and
love him for who he is, just the way You made him. Teach me
to bring out the best in my child, and help him shine his own
light in this world—the light You gave him.
In Jesus's name,
amen.

Shelter from the Storm

I discovered my baby had a personality when he was only
a week old. I had to hold him [in the neonatal intensive
care unit] through the "kangaroo care," where I put on a gown and
held him inside of it with his skin against mine. He cuddled right up
to me, and I could tell that he was going to have an easygoing personality.
—ELIZABETH S.

Each and every one of my children had a different personality
from the start. I have twin sons, and they are very different
from each other. One is a thinker, and one is a doer.
—VICKIE S.

I had a daughter, then had three boys over the next few years. Gender
differences alone were amazing. Even as babies, my boys were much more

active and energetic, and got into a lot more trouble
than my daughter did at their age.

—LISA G.

I knew my baby was unique from day one! I knew she was going
to be emotional like me. She came out of the womb and just poked
her lower lip out as if to say, "You have just ruined my day."

—SUSAN T.

I think every first-time mom panics over all the developmental
milestones: Is my baby rolling over, sitting up, crawling, talking,
and walking on schedule? *But when your second baby comes along,*
you realize those milestones aren't as vital, that each of your
children develops in his own leaps and bounds.

—LIZ G.

FIRST-AID KIT

★ **Worry.** If you're nervous about becoming a mom for the first time
and have no idea what to do with a baby, don't worry. Even
though your baby doesn't come with an instruction manual, you
get something better: God is right beside you, whispering motherhood into your soul.

★ **Discoveries.** Once your baby can crawl, allow her to explore your
home, walking behind her to keep her safe. Take note of what she
likes and where she goes; it will reveal a glimpse of her personality.

★ **Music.** Play different kinds of music for your baby—rock and roll,
classical, and in between. Observe what music he likes best by
watching him move to the rhythm.

★ **Toys.** Lay all her toys out on the carpet and see which ones she plays with first. This will tell you which ones she likes best and offers another insight into her personality.

★ **Friends.** Invite a girlfriend over who has a child your baby's age, and let them play together on the floor. Watch their interaction and see how they play and what they do.

★ **Journal.** Buy a spiral-bound notebook and keep it in a handy place, like a kitchen drawer. When your baby does or says something cute, new, or unique, jot it down. This is a great way to record treasured memories (you can also copy them into his baby book if you have time).

★ **Relax.** Your baby will develop her own personality in her own time; all you need to do is sit back and watch as God shines through her. Don't stress about the little stuff, like missing milestones or keeping the baby book current. Just enjoy being with her.

S.O.S.
(SPIRITUAL OPPORTUNITY TO SAVOR)

For you created my inmost being;
*   you knit me together in my mother's womb.*
I praise you because I am fearfully and wonderfully made;
*   your works are wonderful,*
*   I know that full well.*
My frame was not hidden from you
*   when I was made in the secret place.*
When I was woven together in the depths of the earth,
*   your eyes saw my unformed body.*
All the days ordained for me

were written in your book
before one of them came to be.

PSALM 139:13–16

 Snowflakes and Sisters

When Hannah was born, everyone who saw her said, "She looks just like her daddy!" And she kind of did. Yet she was born with light brown hair and blue eyes, and neither Mike nor I have those.

Then Sydney came along and everyone said, "She looks just like Hannah." And she kind of did. Yet she had a full, thick head of black hair, more like mine, and also had blue eyes.

Even when they were babies, we could see their individual personalities shine through. When Hannah was a baby, she wanted to be held all the time. But Sydney was happiest when we laid her on a blanket on the floor where she could kick her feet.

This year Hannah is twelve (she likes to remind me that she is "almost" a teenager), and Sydney is ten. They have grown into individual people with their own likes and dislikes, ideas and emotions.

Though Mike might like to take credit for their athletic ability and I might want to claim credit for their gift of writing, God made them who they are. He knit them together in my womb, and He knows their days even before they live them. What assurance it is to know that God created our children stitch by stitch and that He knows what their lives will hold!

Just as no two snowflakes are alike, Hannah and Sydney are created to be unique individuals. And they are sisters, sometimes fighting like cats and dogs, driving me crazy. But other times I find them playing with each other or just hanging out and talking girl stuff on the front porch like best friends.

Each of our children is created by God to be unique. One of the biggest challenges of motherhood is accepting them for who they are and realizing that they aren't cookie-cutter versions of us. And one of the biggest blessings is getting a front-row seat to watch them grow into the people God has designed them to be!

Study Questions

1. Does your baby look like you? like your husband?
2. What personality traits can you see developing in your baby?
3. What love language do you speak? does your husband speak?
4. How can you nurture your baby's unique personality?
5. What hopes and dreams do you have for your baby?

Part 3

Living Simply

Loving Life

Monday's Child

Monday's child is fair of face,
Tuesday's child is full of grace,
Wednesday's child is full of woe,
Thursday's child has far to go,
Friday's child is loving and giving,
Saturday's child must work for a living,
But the child that's born on Sunday,
Is fair and wise and good and gay.

Setting Up Base Camp

Organizing Life Around Your Baby

Water from the Word
"Martha, Martha," the Lord answered,
"you are worried and upset about many things,
but only one thing is needed. Mary has chosen what is better,
and it will not be taken away from her."
LUKE 10:41–42

I'm a neatnik through and through—at least that's what my mother called it.

It's really not my fault. I was born with this lifelong disorder that affects every area of my life. But it's a very difficult thing to maintain when there are four aliens—oops, I mean children—constantly invading my space with their stuff. And, boy, do they have a lot of stuff!

My neatnikitis was evident from an early age. I don't know how many times I've heard my mom tell the story about when I was a toddler and first showed symptoms. My dad had just tucked me into my crib for an afternoon nap and had inadvertently left a book out on my nightstand that didn't belong there. (Clearly, I didn't inherit my disorder from him.) Even as a one-year-old, I recognized his blunder and began to cry.

My mom came in and tried rocking me, with no luck. She gave me a bottle, and still I cried. Nothing would calm me. Then she noticed that I kept staring at the book my dad had left on my nightstand. So she put it away, and immediately I fell back to sleep—the peaceful sleep of a neatnik baby.

Space Invaders

Now *I'm* the mom. I'm the one trying to settle the baby down for his afternoon nap.

I'm convinced, however, that none of my kids has inherited my neatnikitis. Such a shame! Being a neatnik is much easier as a toddler than as a mom. Sometimes it feels like my home has been invaded by aliens—four-foot-tall aliens with sticky peanut-butter fingers and jelly-stained faces.

My little space invaders began infiltrating my home even before they could talk or walk. In fact, it began even before they were born—Hannah's things were already cluttering my space while I was pregnant with her. I should probably accept partial blame, since I was the one who bought the battery-operated swing, infant car seat and carrier, bouncy seat, playpen, and jumper. But let's get real here. Did *I* use any of that stuff? Nope. It was all for her.

Food for Thought

The average American receives 49,060 pieces of mail in their lifetime; one-third of it is junk mail. Experts estimate that 80 percent of household congestion—whether in a drawer or closet, on the counter, table or desk, or even the whole room—results from lack of organization rather than insufficient space. Ridding the average home of excess clutter would eliminate 40 percent of the housework.[1]

Extreme Alien Moms

Over the last decade of mothering, I have spent a great deal of time getting to know other moms. They are my species, and like me, they struggle with the clutter of life and the chaos of kids. I have enjoyed lunch at their kitchen tables, played in their backyards, swam in their pools, and through it all, have become friends with some of the most amazing moms that live.

But I have also come to realize that kids are not the only aliens out there. Moms—yep that's you—typically come in alien forms as well. There are basically two extreme alien moms. Most of you probably fall somewhere in the middle, but I'm sure some (like me) fit one description better than the other.

Jumping Jupiters

Jumping Jupiters are neatniks, clean freaks, and often control freaks in other areas of their lives as well.

I'm a Jumping Jupiter mom. Always have been, always will be. My house is never clean enough for me to relax in, and when things are cluttered or dirty, it stresses me out. I am jealous of my girlfriends' homes that always look perfect, and believe me, there are some that do.

Jumping Jupiters tend to have strong personalities, can talk your ear off, and love the smell of Windex in the morning. They can never have enough Murphy Oil Soap in the cupboard, and they love reorganizing their drawers and cabinets.

Some Jumping Jupiters you just love to hate, because their homes are so clean and perfect that it looks as if they are waiting for the nice folks from *Good Housekeeping* to come by for the photo shoot. I have girlfriends who never seem to have a single dust bunny on their floor, no dirty dishes in their sink, and no five-foot-high piles of laundry next to their washing machine.

If we could get away with it, we JJs would kick everyone out of our house just to keep it clean. (Though I've never actually tried that.) We love the scent of Lysol, the sound of a Rubbermaid box snapping shut, and the feel of Pledge between our fingers. *Ahhhhh*. We cringe at the thought of spilled milk, strewn toys, muddy footprints, and carpet crumbs. Our worst enemies are grease and grime, dirt and dust—anything that endangers cleanliness. We detest Polly Pockets, Magnetix balls, and Matchbox cars, all of which were clearly created to torture us. (If you are unfamiliar with Polly, just imagine the smallest dolls with the tiniest clothes and shoes that seem to get lost in every nook and cranny of your space.)

Our allies are boxes, containers, shelves, and anything color-coded or labeled to organize life. We've been known to scream about the importance of folding a quilt in a perfect square before moving it to the drawer, or clamping the open cereal bag shut with a clip before tucking the box top into the slit.

Our best attribute? We are always ready for company. Our homes are like a welcome mat to the world; we love drop-ins.

Nonchalant Neptunes

Nonchalant Neptunes are pack rats, clutter bugs. They are keepers of everything (after all, you never know when might need the December 2001 issue of *Better Homes and Gardens* for that yummy cheesecake recipe you'll never actually make). Neptunes don't mind stepping over a pile of laundry, clean or dirty, or stacks of newspapers to get to the family room. They don't care that they lost the remote control three months ago—they called off the search and simply gave up.

Neptunes are laid-back, relaxed, joyful people. They understand kids' clutter, because they live it. These are the moms who live with piles of stuff that need to be sorted before they decide what to actually do with them, but they never seem to find the time. So when they add their baby's clutter to the mix, it's no big deal; it fits right in.

Food for Thought

RESOURCES FOR BEATING THE CLUTTER OF LIFE

WEB SITES:

www.flylady.com. The Fly Lady Web site offers a host of tips and ideas for getting organized.[2]

www.messies.com. The official site for Messies Anonymous has lots of organizing resources.

www.freecycle.org. This organization aids in de-cluttering by suggesting organizations you can donate to, to help others in need.

BOOKS:

Too Much Stuff: De-Cluttering Your Heart and Home by Kathryn Porter

Organizing for Life: De-Clutter Your Mind to De-Clutter Your World by Sandra Felton

---

A small streak of control freak runs through Neptunes as well: they cringe at the thought of someone else going through their piles, because someone else would *surely* throw away some irreplaceable treasure.

Neptunes' worst enemies include the neverending supply of junk mail, magazines, newspapers, and kids' meal toys (pure evil). Their best allies are busy schedules and active lives that take them away from home, allowing them to forget how messy their house is.

The biggest risk they face is drowning in their own clutter or losing a baby in there somewhere. Their best traits are being so likable that friends will volunteer to come over and help them clean before the baby's first birthday party, and being so joyful that no one minds the chaos.

War of the Worlds

Sometimes staying ahead of the clutter feels more like fighting a war than cleaning a house.

Just the other day, I had regrouped after the battle of the basement but knew there was still one alien unaccounted for. Then I discovered why. He was on laundry basket brigade in my bedroom.

Bam! Explosion in the upper quadrant. His torpedoes exploded and sent clean clothes flying in every direction. My carefully washed and folded laundry was now strewn all over the unvacuumed bedroom carpet.

What to do now? Time to surrender and escort the guilty alien down to watch a thirty-minute video. This would allow me much-needed time to regroup and prepare for the next alien attack.

It is exhausting, fighting the war on mess with aliens aboard my ship. It's like living with the enemy. And my options seem limited.

Option No. 1: Staple my child's pants to the carpet and play videos for eight hours straight. Yes, I might get the laundry washed, folded, and put away in the same day, but eight hours of television—even *Veggie Tales*—might fry their little brains.

Option No. 2: Give my children 100 percent of my attention 100 percent of the time. They would be thrilled, and I might even win a Mother of the Year award. The main problem? We would never eat a home-cooked meal or wear clean clothes again. And I would have to buy a backhoe to clear a path through the clutter that would develop.

I'm not sure I have the strength to win this war. There must be a different battle plan. A compromise.

Discovering What Truly Matters

I always thought that, as a mom, I was the teacher. I was there to instruct and guide my children in the way they should grow and mature over their lifetime. But sometimes I learn more from them than they learn from me—especially about what truly matters in life.

On one particularly busy day, I was trying to get supper prepared, and I practically pierced my big toe on a Polly Pocket doll. I was already grumpy—I'd had little sleep the night before because baby Riley decided to throw an all-night slumber party. As pain shot through my foot, I shouted at Sydney, "Pick up your things and put them away!"

Sydney looked up at me with tears in her big blue eyes. "Mommy," she whimpered, "I was waiting for you to play with me."

Bam. Shot fired. Direct hit to my heart.

I sank down onto the cold kitchen linoleum and suddenly realized how selfish I had been that day. I hadn't spent a single minute playing with Sydney. I was checking off my to-do list in battle mode, fighting alien interference with my agenda. In the blink of an eye, I suddenly understood how this was affecting my daughter.

I held out my arms, and Sydney crawled up into my lap to snuggle. She put her skinny arms around my neck, squeezed as tightly as she could, and cried. "I'm sorry, Mommy. I'll pick them up."

Bam. Second shot fired. Now the guilt was sinking in.

So I did what any alien mom would do. I took a deep breath, closed my eyes, and held on tight. Sydney whispered, "Mommy, will you play Polly with me?"

My heart melted. I had been running so fast, keeping up such a pace, that I had forgotten who I was. I may be a neatnik at heart, but God made me a mom.

In that moment, I let go of my agenda. Cleaning the house was not as important as spending time with Sydney. I hugged her tight and told her I loved her. Then we sat in the middle of the kitchen and played Polly Pocket.

Surrendering to Their Stuff

At the drop of a dust rag, my beautiful aliens will be grown and heading off to college, marriage, and their own lives. So will yours.

Our time with our children is limited. There are only so many opportunities for a mother to read *If You Give a Mouse a Cookie,* only so many good-night kisses and bedtime prayers to distribute, only so many "Mommy, would you play Polly with me?" moments before they're gone.

This Jumping Jupiter has experienced a change of heart. I've let go of the need to keep my space perfectly clean. I not only surrendered the battle; I surrendered the war. I accept the fact that aliens live in my space. I've decided they're not the enemy; they are the heroes. After all, they taught me what is truly important—making my house into a home.

So now their stuff is in my family room, and it's starting to look like a Nonchalant Neptune lives here. There are even toys in the kitchen— a few Pollys on the floor. But my children have a more relaxed and joyful mom. A mom who runs at their pace and plays in their space.

What's a Respectable Alien Mom to Do?

Some of you identify as either a Jumping Jupiter or a Nonchalant Neptune, but most of you share some traits of both—depending on the day of the week and whether or not the laundry is done. Each of us, no matter where we fall on the mom-alien spectrum, needs to adapt our lives and our homes to motherhood.

Task No. 1: Accept Who You Are

Whether you are a Jumping Jupiter, a Nonchalant Neptune, or some-one in between, you are who you are. Be thankful for your strengths and work to accept and improve your weaknesses. Know that God cre-ated *you* to be the perfect mom for your children; you are exactly what they need.

Task No. 2: Realize That Babies Add Clutter

Accept the fact that children (and men) add clutter to your life. Your home will probably never look the same again—at least not for the next twenty years or so.

Task No. 3: Set Realistic Goals

Set realistic standards for your home. Know that stepping on a cracker or two will not damage your foot (although a sharp plastic toy might). Likewise, if you are a Nonchalant Neptune, you need to locate your sweeper, which is probably packed away in its original box or gathering dust in your basement.

Making Your House a Home

Remember that whether you are a Jumping Jupiter or a Nonchalant Neptune, you are first and foremost a mom. Find what works for you and then focus on enjoying your life. The most important thing is not whether your kitchen floors are clean; it's that your children feel loved and your house feels like a H-O-M-E.

H—Have heaven as your model.

"In my Father's house are many rooms; if it were not so, I would have told you. I am going there to prepare a place for you" (John 14:2).

O—Open your doors for visitors.
Share with God's people who are in need. Practice hospitality (Romans 12:13).

M—Make your house feel lived-in and cozy.
"Do not store up for yourselves treasures on earth, where moth and rust destroy, and where thieves break in and steal" (Matthew 6:19).

E—Establish love first.
"A new command I give you: Love one another. As I have loved you, so you must love one another" (John 13:34).

Now get ready for the invasion! Life as a mom is a wild ride, and you're going to live with these little space invaders for the next two decades. But I promise that you'll learn to love your little aliens, clutter and all.

FAITH ON FIRE

Dear Lord,
You made me a mom, no matter how cluttered or clean my house is. Help me make our house into a home that is filled with joy and laughter, love and grace. Teach me to find the balance between living in the moment with my kids and organizing and cleaning my house. And when I lose sight of who I am, remind me that I'm first and foremost a mom.
In Jesus's name,
amen.

Shelter from the Storm

One day while heating baby food in the microwave, I discovered that I could wipe out the kitchen sink during the twenty seconds of wait time. Then I realized it takes me just four minutes to make a bed. You may not be able to clean your house top to bottom, but you can squeeze out that kind of time.

—ERIN S.

I found I can do lots of things with one hand and even with my toes—I can work the TV remote with my feet now.

—ALLISON L.

Don't stress about all the small stuff. Try to enjoy each moment you have with your children. When they are older, you can teach them to help you clean up, and then it will be a team effort.

—SUE W.

Learn to relax your housecleaning standards. Don't try to get straight As; aim for Cs.

—ERIN S.

FIRST-AID KIT

Clutter-Busting Ideas

- **Toy storage.** Keep colorful crates under your coffee table for toy storage. Cleaning up is as easy as tossing them in and shoving them under the table.
- **Toy chest.** Put a large toy chest in your family room so toys are accessible and easy to put away.

- **Papers.** Hang an inexpensive bulletin board in your kitchen. Tack up important numbers, forms, or documents so you don't lose them.

- **Coatrack.** Place a coatrack in the entryway of your home and teach everyone to hang his own jacket or coat up when he comes in the door. You can shop for an inexpensive coatrack online or make your own. Have a lumberyard cut a piece of oak one foot by four feet and bevel the edge; then stain the wood and screw on sturdy brass hooks.

- **Laundry.** Do what works for your schedule. You can wash a load before bed, put it in the dryer in the morning, and put the clothes away after lunch. Or declare one day a week laundry day, and get it all done then.

- **Junk mail.** Get rid of all junk mail immediately. Store bills in a bill organizer where you can see them and will be reminded to pay them.

- **A task a day.** Plan one chore for each day and write it on your calendar: Monday, mop the floor. Tuesday, run the sweeper.

- **Shelves.** Get a bookshelf or curio cabinet for all those tiny prized items you don't want broken by toddlers.

- **Stairs.** Keep a basket at the bottom of the stairs for things that need to go up and one at the top for things that need to go down. Unload the basket every morning and evening so it doesn't become overwhelming.

S.O.S.
(SPIRITUAL OPPORTUNITY TO SAVOR)

Do not let your hearts be troubled. Trust in God; trust also in me. In my Father's house are many rooms; if it were not so, I would have told you. I am going there to prepare a place for

you. And if I go and prepare a place for you, I will come back
and take you to be with me that you also may be where I am.
You know the way to the place where I am going.

JOHN 14:1–4

 ## What Makes a House a Home?

When Mike and I were first married, we lived on the bottom floor of a two-story duplex. A young, single mom lived in the apartment above us with her little toddler. At nighttime, we could hear that little girl run from the front of the house to the back time and time again. *Boom, boom, boom.* It sounded like a herd of elephants had moved in and was on the run.

Our kitchen was this awful, bright peach color, and the floor was slanted; walking across it was like going downhill. The carpets were old, the paint was faded, and a musty smell permeated everything.

But we loved that old house. It was our home.

After two years of living in what Mike calls the "city," we moved to the two-hundred-acre farm where Mike grew up. There were two houses on the farm, and his parents lived in one of them. Mike's grandma had just left the older house and gone into a nursing home, so it sat empty. Mike's parents offered it to us, and we decided to "go country."

Our old farmhouse had a yellow kitchen with green carpeting and red countertops. There was purple shag carpeting in our bedroom, and the walls were done in 1970s paneling. The windows wouldn't all open, there was no central air, and everything squeaked or creaked.

But we loved that old house. It was our home.

Making a house into a home has a lot more to do with how you live than what it looks like. Is there love in your family? Do you find the joy in each day? Are you thankful for what you have? Have you invited Jesus into your house? into your life?

In the book of John, Jesus tells us not to worry but instead to trust in God. He also tells us that in His Father's house, there are many rooms and that He is going there to prepare a place for us.

But while we are still on earth, it is up to us to make our house a home. It doesn't really matter if you live in a mansion or an apartment, or even if your carpets are lime green. How we live in our earthly homes will show our children what our heavenly home will be like.

Study Questions

1. What do you like about your house?
2. When was the last time you thanked God for your house?
3. Do you feel jealous when you visit your friends' homes?
4. What can you do to make your house more homey?

Coordinated Efforts

Meeting Your Family's Needs

Water from the Word
God will meet all your needs according to
his glorious riches in Christ Jesus.
PHILIPPIANS 4:19

I remember walking home from kindergarten, down the road from the bus stop to our red ranch house near the woods. It always seemed like a long distance for my little legs to walk. But the moment I opened our front door and smelled my cheese sandwich grilling, I knew I was home—and I knew Mom was there.

My mother has a master's degree and worked as a social worker for many years. But as a kid, I didn't care about that; I cared only that she was there making my lunch after the long walk home from the bus stop. I only cared that she was my mom.

That's how kids think. That's how they feel.

My Grandma Knoedler was a registered nurse way back before it was common for women to work full-time. She even helped support her family through the Depression when my grandpa wasn't able to find a job. Grandma was a woman ahead of her time, and she raised my mom to believe that she could have a career, a marriage, and a family.

Mom came of age in the sixties during an era in which women fought for rights, protested, and pushed for fulfillment in career, not family. But as much as my mom wanted a career, she wanted to be a mom even more. She always put her job behind motherhood, sometimes working night shifts or in private practice, sometimes working part-time.

My mother and my grandmother both had a great impact on my life. In a million different ways, they influenced my mothering and career choices. Many of the decisions I make can be attributed to those two very strong women.

Day-Care Dilemma

While I was going to college, I worked at the day-care facility on campus. We watched faculty and staff children—from six-week-old babies through preschool-age children. Most of my time was spent in the preschool room, but I spent time in the infant and toddler rooms too.

I will never forget the experience of simultaneously feeding six babies their lunch. First, I lined them all up in their highchairs. Then I went down the line over and over, doling out cut-up hot dogs, crackers, and sippy cups filled with milk. I would coo for a bit to one, and then move on to the next baby.

It was assembly-line mothering at best, and even as a twenty-year-old I was bothered by it.

This particular day care was considered one of the best in the state. It was a clean and modern facility, the staff was well trained, and it adhered to state guidelines for child-to-teacher ratios. But something inside me felt desperately sad for these children. Many were dropped off at 7 a.m. and picked up at 6 p.m. They spent their entire day with us, not their moms or dads. I knew this system had to have some sort of long-term impact on them, but I had no idea how great it might be.

Right now some of you might be feeling guilty, discouraged, disappointed, frustrated, or even downright angry with me. For many of you who have your children in day care, this is a difficult chapter to read.

Let me first reassure you that I do not want to heap any guilt on you. Moms deal with enough guilt daily. Let me also reassure you that you are the mom your children need, and that God is guiding you in your mothering.

As I stated, this is probably one of the toughest decisions you will make as a mom, and each of you has to make the decision that works best for you and your family. In my opinion, one of the following options is best for your children: staying at home and not working, working part-time, or working from home. But the most important thing is to prioritize your children, whether you work or not.

With that in mind, if you do work full-time and are in need of day care, you can also find quality child care that will bless your family.

Choice Number 1

I believe if you work full-time, the best option might be to have a baby-sitter come to your home and watch your children. But this can be a fairly expensive route. Grandparents sometimes are able to help out here, taking a day or two each week to help cut down your costs and have special bonding time with their grandchildren.

My sister-in-law, Mary Beth, is a registered nurse. She and her husband, Chad, both work outside the home. They have two boys under three. Chad owns a business with his dad and Mary Beth works at a local hospital. Together they have found a way to raise their boys. Chad takes the boys to work one day, and Chad's mom comes down to baby-sit one day. Mary Beth then works afternoons and evenings when Chad can be home with the boys.

Choice Number 2

Another fantasic option would be to find a licensed in-home day care in your neighborhood. It's best if there are only a few children and you know the babysitter and her family.

Krista, a friend of mine, is a kindergarten teacher who works half days and is a busy mom raising two boys under five. She's at home in the morning and then in the afternoon takes the boys to a woman who runs a day care from her home. It's a win-win for all.

Choice Number 3

A local day-care facility that is licensed and one that ranks well on the child-teacher ratios can be a solid option for working moms. The day-care center should meet or exceed all state and federal standards, and you should be able to "pop in" any time of day on any day of the week. And you really should pop in unannounced on occasion. For more information about licensing for your state and a listing of day cares in your area, see www.daycare.com.

 Food for Thought

An estimated 12 million American infants, toddlers, and preschoolers—more than half of all children in this age group—attend day care. The majority of these kids spend close to forty hours per week in day care; many start when they are only weeks old.

About 26 percent of children who spend more than forty-five hours per week in day care go on to have serious behavioral problems in kindergarten. By contrast, only 10 percent of kids who spend less than ten hours per week in day care have comparable problems.[1]

Little Girls and Big Dreams

My mom taught me to reach for the stars. As a little girl, I dreamed of big careers in this field or that, of traveling the globe and living in a big city full of lights and a nightlife that went on well past dark. To be completely honest, being a stay-at-home mom never figured into my future.

I graduated from college and, with my mom's full support, enrolled immediately in graduate school. When Mike and I married in 1992, I still planned to pursue a busy, important career in marketing.

I never gave much thought to what I would do with my baby if I did work. When I became pregnant with Hannah in 1995, it was as if I had been hit in the head with a boulder. Who would care for her while Mike and I both worked full-time? Who would hold her, hug her, feed her, and snuggle with her on those cold winter days when the snowdrifts were higher than our front porch?

Mike and I both knew things needed to change. I was working full-time as a marketing manager in real estate, and I was teaching college courses several nights a week. That left precious few extra hours for my marriage or for motherhood.

Food for Thought

FROM A 2004 SEGMENT OF *60 MINUTES*:

"Could it really be that this generation of women, the first to achieve success without having to fight for it, is now walking away, willingly, and without regrets? Census bureau statistics show a 15 percent increase in the number of stay-at-home moms in less than ten years."[2] And many of these women are walking away from high-powered careers to be moms.

Mike never pushed or cajoled me into quitting my job. Together, we looked at our options, and together we decided that I could teach college part-time, two evenings a week, and that Mike would provide the main source of income for our family.

It was not an easy decision, and I know many of you are struggling with those same questions and concerns. I encourage you to pray about it, talk about it, and crunch the numbers. You might be amazed at what you can live without if you get to be the one raising your baby.

I get to be the mom. And that is the best blessing of all.

Perhaps you've been wondering how in the world I find time to write, teach college, and be a mom. Well, the first thing I did was cut back on my teaching. I only teach one or two evenings a week in the fall and spring, and I never teach in the summer months. Most of my writing is done while my three older children are in school and my toddler is napping, or late at night when everyone is sleeping. Some writing takes place during the summer months when Mike (a teacher) is able to be home full-time with the kids. And sometimes I write with a toddler pulling on my arm, wanting to snuggle on the couch, which leads me to a needed break from my work and reminds me why I work from home in the first place.

The Mommy Wars

There is a heated debate raging over whether women should work or stay home. Women everywhere believe passionately in their choice. We are all guilty of judging women who make decisions that don't align with our philosophy. We put each other down. We declare war on the moms who aren't doing what they "should" be doing.

It breaks my heart to see many women drawing battle lines over motherhood. As moms, we need to end the war that's raging between career and stay-at-home moms. In fact, I'm convinced that the only difference is between moms who prioritize their kids and those who don't—working or not.

Food for Thought

Stay-at-home moms typically work a 91.6-hour work week at their job. That's a lot of overtime!

Working moms work 44 hours at their job and another 49.8 hours at home as a mom. That totals 93.8 hours a week.

In today's market, if paid, stay-at-home-moms would earn $134,121 a year, and working moms would earn $85,876 for the "mom" portion of their jobs.

Find out what YOU are worth, just for fun. Visit http://swz.salary.com/momsalarywizard/htmls/mswl_momcenter.html and create your own "Mom paycheck" with the Mom Salary Wizard.[3]

I know some stay-at-home mothers who don't work outside the home at all but who volunteer on or attend so many church committees, community boards, Bible studies, and women's groups that they may as well be working full-time! I also know working moms who sacrifice sleep, time spent with their husbands, and pampering themselves, so they can devote every extra minute to their children.

If you work full-time outside your home, the last thing I want to do is add guilt to your life. But I do encourage you to seek balance in a way that prioritizes your children. It's important to remember that whether you're a stay-at-home mom, work part-time, or have a full-time career, you are first and foremost a mom.

The Balancing Act

I don't know if there is a perfect solution, but I do know there is a workable one. Life is about choices. And each choice brings with it a price tag, a sacrifice—something that must be given up or postponed.

With my MBA in marketing, I could be working for a high-powered firm, furthering my career, and earning a solid salary. But I choose for now to put that career on the back burner, because I found one that fits better with motherhood: teaching part-time and writing.

It's all about timing. When your children are young, they need you home during the day. When they are school-age, they need you home in the afternoons and evenings. You can find a job that allows you to be there when they need you. Yes, it is exhausting, but it is possible.

I also understand some moms don't have an option. Divorced, single, widowed, or in a tragic circumstance, they *must* work full-time to pay the bills. I feel for those moms and pray that they find the help they need to get through the difficult years of mothering.

But more often, I see moms who could stay home but choose instead to work full-time in order to maintain a certain lifestyle: two cars, a big house, new furniture, summer vacations, Colorado ski trips, new clothes, and dinners out. Those are all wonderful things, but each of us has to decide whether they are worth the price tag.

Mike and I have found a way to live on his high-school math teacher's income. I drive a newer minivan, but Mike drives a 1986 Jeep that's about to top 200,000 miles (a fact Mike is rather proud of). We take simple vacations with our kids, including church family camp and weekends spent at my parents' cottage on Lake Erie. We don't eat out very often, and I buy a lot of clothes on clearance, at secondhand stores, and at Goodwill.

I'm not complaining. We have a great life, and I wouldn't change a

> ### Food for Thought
> When moms join the work force, up to 68 percent of their income goes for work-related expenses, such as child care, transportation, taxes, and lunch money.[4]
>
> In just twenty-five years, American families have been radically restructured as the number of women in the work force has nearly doubled.[5]

thing about it. It's simply a reflection of the choices we have made, and we have no regrets. We budget and sacrifice, as do most families. We may not vacation in exotic locales or eat out at fancy restaurants, but we have four kids who know they come first in our lives. And we hope that they will grow up to someday put their own kids first.

Career Sequencing

Being a mom isn't necessarily about giving up your career. Rather, it's about sequencing your career—taking it one step at a time, making one decision at a time.

After all, life as a mom isn't stagnant. It changes shape over the years. During the baby and toddler stages, you're needed at home. But once your children start attending school, there are certain hours during the day when you can squeeze work in. For me, that's usually from 8 a.m. to 3 p.m.

And don't forget that you have a partner. Your husband may also want to make career adjustments. Perhaps you could work part-time while your kids are young, increasing your hours as they grow older and start school. You may choose to put your career on hold for motherhood, or you could work first shift and your husband third. Between the two of you, you can be available to your children.

Perhaps you're shaking your head right now, thinking, *There's no way we can afford that!* My experience tells me this: if you want it to happen, you can make it happen.

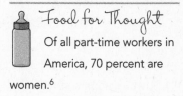

Food for Thought

Of all part-time workers in America, 70 percent are women.[6]

Among all part-time workers, 64.1 percent of them worked full-time before cutting back, and almost a third (31.3 percent) had been home with children.[7]

The reason given for going part-time for 60.3 percent of workers was making family their priority.[8]

Thanks to technology and access to information, there are many things women can do from home.

Of course, you alone must determine how much extra energy you can devote to working, because as we all know, motherhood is exhausting. I remember one particular summer when my babies were young and our finances were tight. I decided to teach several extra classes at another local university—a total of five classes in one semester.

Mike was home that summer and played Mr. Mom, but kids aren't fools. There are times when they simply want Mom. No substitute—no matter how charming and loving—will do. At the end of the day I had very little left to give Mike or the kids, and we all paid a price. It was a tough lesson to learn, and I have never taken on as intense a teaching schedule again.

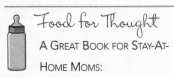

Food for Thought
A GREAT BOOK FOR STAY-AT-HOME MOMS:
Home-Alone America: The Hidden Toll of Day Care, Behavioral Drugs, and Other Parent Substitutes by Mary Eberstadt
A GREAT BOOK FOR WORKING MOMS:
The Frazzled Factor by Karol Ladd and Jane Jarrell

Now Hannah is twelve and Sydney is ten. They have activities after school, and I am once again adjusting my career to accommodate their schedule. Recently, I cut back on teaching and increased my writing.

That's career sequencing. That's motherhood.

Your Choice

Only you know what your kids need from you, and only you know how to make it happen.

So pray about your choices, talk to your husband, and then find a way to make it work for you. But no matter what decision you come to, place your kids at the top of the daily priority list. And remember that if things don't work out, down the road you can always make a *new* choice.

FAITH ON FIRE

Dear Lord,

Becoming a mom turned my world upside down, and sometimes it's difficult to find my way, get my balance back. But You have blessed me with this precious child, and I'm the only one on earth who can be his mom. I know the decision to go back to work, to stay home, or to find middle ground is probably one of the toughest decisions I will make. Help me prioritize my family, put my own needs aside, and partner with my husband to make the best decision we can in our circumstances. I know You will provide for us and meet all our needs however You see fit.

In Jesus's name,

amen.

Shelter from the Storm

My son is only five weeks old, but already he has changed me. Things I used to care about pale in comparison to caring for him. I'm less concerned about my ambition and more content knowing I'm working hard at raising a young man.

—ALLISON L.

Having experienced life both as a working mother of a newborn and as a stay-at-home mother with my second baby, I believe that sometimes God calls mothers to the workplace and sometimes to the home.

That doesn't make the working mother better or worse than the stay-at-home mother. Each individual is called to obedience in his or her circumstances. And if we respond in obedience to God, He'll bless us.
—LORI S.

We have the best of both worlds. We purchased a larger home with my parents, so our son would be surrounded by family. My husband and I both work full-time, as does my dad. My mom is home full-time and helps care for my nine-year-old son after school until we get home.
—NANN W.

It is exhausting trying to work at my job and be a mom. But when Ethan puts his arms around my neck, it's all worth it.
—MARY BETH D.

FIRST-AID KIT

★ **Budget.** Make one list of all earned family income and a second of all expenses. Create one version with your income as a working mom and one without. See if you can swing it financially.

★ **Changes.** Think about what you can live without that you currently take for granted. Think about forgoing a new car, vacations, eating out, new clothes. Then redo your budget minus those items and see how the numbers crunch.

★ **Talk.** Talk to your husband about your desire to be a stay-at-home mom and see if he has any ideas on how you can swing it. This should be a team decision, and it requires a team effort.

★ **Part-time.** If you wish to continue working part-time, think creatively about what jobs you would enjoy. If you are a businesswoman, you might consider starting a business from home. If you are a teacher, try substitute teaching a couple of days a week or tutoring elementary students in the evenings. Be creative and weigh the time spent away from home against what is best for your baby.

★ **Swing shift**. If you must work full-time, try switching to evenings or weekends when your husband can be with the baby. Just don't forget that you were husband and wife before you became Mom and Dad. You'll need to make time for each other through these exhausting years to keep your marriage strong.

★ **Day care**. If you work, think about hiring a sitter to come to your home, or take your child to an in-home baby-sitter. Grandmas are the best choice, but it's very important not to take advantage of them; if they baby-sit for you full-time, you should be paying them.

★ **Pray**. Whatever you decide, keep God at the center of your decision. Know that if the situation isn't working, you can change your plans down the road. Be flexible and open to adjustment.

S.O.S.
(Spiritual Opportunity to Savor)

Children, obey your parents in the Lord, for this is right.
"Honor your father and mother"—which is the first com-
mandment with a promise—"that it may go well with you
and that you may enjoy long life on the earth."

Fathers, do not exasperate your children; instead, bring
them up in the training and instruction of the Lord.

Ephesians 6:1–4

Exasperation Abounds

When Hannah was an only child, I thought mothering was stressful and exhausting. I would actually get a baby-sitter (usually Grandma or Grandpa) to come over and stay with her so I could go grocery shopping or run errands without her on my hip.

I guess it's all in your perspective. I was a new mom back then, and just getting around with a baby—in and out of the car, in and out of the store—was exhausting. More than a dozen years later, I now have four kids stressing me out. And do you know what? I cherish the times when I only have to take *one* of them to the grocery store.

Motherhood is exhausting. It is stressful. It can exasperate you in the blink of an eye if you aren't careful. And when we get exasperated, what do we do? Well, I can only speak for myself, but I tend to *yell*!

Yep, I can raise my voice and yell as loud as a ringmaster in a circus: "Hannah, why is your shirt lying on the floor?" "Sydney...*stop* fighting with your brother!"

Kids will be kids, babies will be babies, and toddlers...well, they'll get into everything. Siblings fight. Milk spills. Get over it.

When I am exhausted, run-down, and stressed out about life, that's when I yell. The kids have good days and bad, but it really boils down to me and my attitude. If I am running too fast, trying to get too much of *my* stuff done, or have too much on my plate, I get overwhelmed and I yell.

Believe me, as good as it can feel to let loose and bellow, it never accomplishes anything positive. In fact, it serves to teach my children to yell when they themselves are mad.

God tells us in the book of Ephesians that children should obey their parents. But hold on to your hat—He also tells us not to "exasperate" our children. It's a two-way street, Mom. As you strive to bring your children up in the Christian faith, remember that you need to slow your life down. You need to check your attitude, take a deep breath, and *stop yelling*!

Study Questions

1. When was the last time your baby or older child frustrated you? What did they do?
2. How do you react to life's stresses when you are exhausted and stressed out?
3. How do you react to life's stresses when you are well rested and in a good mood?
4. Do you think our joy should come from our circumstances? Why or why not?
5. List three things you can do to slow your life down. What could you give up? Would it be worth it?

Exploring New Territory

Making Room for the In-Laws

Water from the Word

*For this reason a man will leave his father and mother
and be united to his wife, and they will become one flesh.*

GENESIS 2:24

Mike and I had been dating for only a few weeks when I drove more than two hours with a college girlfriend to watch him play football for the Baldwin-Wallace Yellow Jackets. I had never been to one of his games before, and I had no idea what kind of surprise lay in store.

Throughout the game, my girlfriend, Mandy, and I sat on the sidelines cheering for the Yellow Jackets football team as we watched Mike, number 68, play defense. After the game, I decided to drop by the end zone and say hello to Mike. Mandy didn't want to tag along, so she left to wait in the car. As I made my way through the crowd, I caught Mike's eye. He came over and gave me a hug; I kissed his cheek. Then he led me to a huge circle of people and began introducing me. His mom, his dad, and his sisters were there, along with a lot of extended family members and friends.

I began to feel a little lightheaded. My knees buckled, and I thought

I might pass out. I couldn't believe Mike had so much family coming to watch him play football! It seemed like the entire state of Ohio was there to cheer him on. It was overwhelming, to say the least, especially for a girl from a small family.

As soon as Mike introduced me, he took off to chat with a buddy. Yep, just like a guy! He left me there all alone with that huge crowd of people I had just met. We laugh about it now, but at the time it wasn't funny at all. Everyone was staring at me as though I had green hair and flames coming out of my mouth. I think I managed to make successful small talk for about ten seconds before making my escape back to Mandy.

As you may have guessed, Mike comes from a large and very close-knit family. He has three sisters and more cousins than I can count. He grew up on a farm in a rural area—think Mayberry meets *The Waltons*. Most of his aunts, uncles, cousins, and second cousins live in the same county. But as big as his family is, he is still an only son. I think this presented a challenge for Mike's mom, Mary Ann, when we married. And for me as his wife.

 Food for Thought

TO ACHIEVE A BETTER RELATIONSHIP WITH YOUR IN-LAWS

Mothers-in-law: Don't criticize your daughter-in-law's homemaking or mothering techniques.

Sons/husbands: Be supportive of your spouse and understanding of your mother.

Daughters-in-law: Set preestablished boundaries about things like visits and expectations.[1]

My mother-in-law, Mary Ann, is a truly beautiful person inside and out, and we have grown to love each other over the years—and not just because I married her son. We truly like and respect each other. My father-in-law, Jerry, still considers me a city girl, but I'm slowly gaining "farm girl" credibility with each passing year.

We have settled into a comfortable relationship, perhaps because we live in closer quarters than most: In 1999, Mike and I bought and renovated the century-old farmhouse that Jerry grew up in. My in-laws live on the same farm, about a half-mile up the hill. That's right, my in-laws are our next-door neighbors.

Trail Mix, Sugar Cookies, and Grandparents

When I was a little girl, I loved making the long drive to my Grandma Knoedler's house. Because she lived adjacent to a golf course, Grandma had a great sledding hill in her backyard. We would sled for hours on that hill. Sometimes she threw on her red winter coat and mismatched hat and gloves and came sledding with us. Most of the time, however, she stayed indoors and made us old-fashioned hot cocoa (with milk, of course)—the perfect treat to warm our souls and our feet.

When it was time to go home, she would go to the cupboard under her sink and pull out her signature bags of trail mix or sugar cookies. They were sweet treats to remind us of her love and make the long ride home more enjoyable.

Grandparents play vital roles in every child's life. But because they are also our parents and our in-laws, things can get complicated. According to Bible scholar and teacher Kenneth W. Howard, "Family relationships are vital and important to any marriage, including the relationship with parents and in-laws. But there are some adjustments and restrictions that must be made."[2] In fact, studies show that in-law problems rank first or second as problems in both new and long-term marriages.

Most of the time, this conflict is between the women in the family—that is, the wife and her mother-in-law.

Mike's mother, Mary Ann, grew up on a farm in a small rural Ohio town, whereas I grew up in the suburbs of Cleveland. She was the head cheerleader and homecoming queen in high school; I was the point guard on our girls' basketball team. I'm probably not the kind of girl Mary Ann pictured Mike marrying. But God had different plans, I guess. Besides, it goes both ways—I doubt my parents ever pictured me marrying a baseball coach and living on a beef cattle farm!

Celebrate the Differences

When you take your vows, you don't marry just your husband, you marry his family as well. How do two completely different families successfully come together? It can be challenging, but the secret lies in showing genuine love and respect for each other.

In many traditional wedding ceremonies, the bride and the groom each take a single candle and together light a larger unity candle, signifying their becoming one. Then they blow out the first two candles. That tradition seems off to me, because you don't lose your family of origin when you marry. And though the unity candle is a

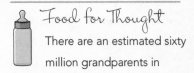

Food for Thought
There are an estimated sixty million grandparents in America. More than 80 percent are in at least monthly contact with their grandchildren, while roughly 25 percent provide essential child care for their grandchildren.[3]

sweet symbol of unity in marriage, I think a better representation might be to leave the two individual candles burning. This would be an apt reflection of the love, support, faith, and encouragement of the parents, in-laws, and siblings who remain a very big part of our lives.

You now have a family that is larger than before. And just like the family you came from, things won't always be peaches and cream. Family is about loving one another as is and respecting the differences we have. It's about being there for one another through thick and thin.

You don't have to be like your mother-in-law, you are two different people. But you do need to find a way to fit her into your family's life and make her feel loved. After all, she is grandma to your children, and that will have an impact for generations yet to come.

Men Aren't Immune

Women are not the only ones who struggle with their in-laws. Things went fairly smoothly for Mike and my parents until Hannah was born; then everything changed. (In fact, Mike thought I should call this chapter "Keep Your Hands Off My Baby!")

Mike was a hands-on dad from the start. He was the best diaper-changing dad there ever was, and he could settle a fussy, crying Hannah down when nothing else worked. Shortly after Hannah's birth, we made our first trip to my parents' house. Turns out it was very difficult for Mike to let anybody else hold Hannah. If my mom went to take Hannah from him, he would shoot me a look from across the room that clearly said, *Is she seriously going to take* my *baby out of* my *arms? Just who does she think* she *is?*

To Mike's credit, he gritted his teeth and

 Food for Thought

SEVEN RULES FOR DEALING WITH IN-LAWS

1. Develop your own independence.
2. Keep your marriage private.
3. Consider your in-laws' concerns legitimate.
4. Accept your in-laws' weaknesses.
5. Make an effort to be their friend.
6. Treat them like you want to be treated.
7. Allow God to be a partner in your marriage.[4]

let Hannah's excited new maternal grandparents dote on her. But he kept very close watch on the situation.

Boy, do things change with baby number two. When Sydney was born two years later, it didn't faze Mike at all to have my parents hold her. In fact, by then he considered it a welcome relief to pass her off to them for a moment or two. Had they become better grandparents? No. Mike simply learned to relax and trust them.

Letters from the Heart

Sometimes I express myself best through letter writing. For this reason, I wanted to write one letter to you and another to your mother-in-law. Feel free to share these with each other. I pray they bring love, joy, and laughter into your family.

Dear Daughter-in-Law,

It is tough to feel like an outsider, the one who never seems to fit in or say the right thing at your husband's family gatherings. Perhaps you sometimes feel jealous of the love your husband has for his mom and of the bond they share.

You want to make sure you come first in your husband's heart and in his life, but you have to realize that you hold all the cards here: you are his wife, the mother of his children, the controller of the calendar, the keeper of all things precious to him.

Please know that your mother-in-law also sometimes feels left out, as if you have forgotten that she was the one who loved your husband first, and raised him to be the man you chose to marry.

And he is wonderful, you know. Full of character and kindness, strength and determination. He loves the Lord, and he loves you, probably more than you will ever fully realize.

*Have you ever taken the time to thank your mother-in-law
for raising her son to be a godly man, the man you married?
Have you ever told her you love her not just because she is his
mom, but because she is your mom?*

*And she is also a grandmother to your children. The one
who whispers love into their hearts with kisses and cookies. So
give your mother-in-law a break. Forgive her for any stepped-on
toes over the years. Know that she not only loves her son; she
loves you as well. And accept her love, however it is given, for
exactly what it is—love from a mother to a daughter.*

Sincerely,

A daughter-in-law just like you

Dear Mother-in-Law,

*I know you occasionally feel like an outsider, like one who no longer
seems to fit in your son's family. Perhaps you sometimes feel jealous of the
love your son has for his wife and of the bond they share.*

*At one time you came first in your son's life; now his wife does. You
were once his confidante, and now she is. When he was a little boy, you
were his whole universe—the one he proposed marriage to a hundred
times. You hung the moon and the stars. You had all the answers. Now she
is there, taking your place.*

*No matter how old he gets, he will always be your little boy in over-
alls and bare feet holding a muddy frog in his hands, asking if he can keep
it as a pet. But to her, he is a man. The man of her dreams.*

*You did a wonderful job, Mom, raising your son to be a man of
character and strength, a man who loves the Lord and loves his wife. You
should be proud of the man he has become, and know that he is proud of
the mom you are.*

Your daughter-in-law wants you to love her, to respect her as his wife, to approve of her. After all, she loves your son more than the moon and the stars. So rest easy, dear Mom, and know that you have done your job well. No one has forgotten your place in his life. Just be sure to scoot over and let his wife stand next to him.

Sincerely,

A loving daughter-in-law

FAITH ON FIRE

Dear Lord,

I came into marriage as a unique individual with a different background from my husband. Our differences make us stronger, but our differences also make it difficult at times for our families to come together.

Help me respect my husband's family, history, and background. Help me forgive my mother-in-law for anything she says or does that hurts my feelings, and please forgive me for hurting her feelings. Help us to love, respect, and appreciate each other. I know I take my in-laws for granted at times and that I'm not always the daughter-in-law You want me to be. Guide and lead me. In Jesus's name,

amen.

Shelter from the Storm

Whenever my mother-in-law is around, I tense up. I get nervous that she is judging me. I know everything I say and do is under her scrutiny, and it bothers me that I never seem to measure up to her standards.

—JOY B.

*I tried for years to befriend my sister-in-law.
As hard as I worked at it, she never seemed to want to be
friends with me. So I finally came to my senses and gave up.
And what I discovered is that we could be sisters-in-law
without being friends. We could love and respect each other
without having the added pressure of trying to be friends.*

—AMY D.

*My husband doesn't seem to stand up to his parents when they
do something that hurts my feelings. I wish he would stand up for me.*

—MARY T.

*I have two sisters-in-law, and they are very close.
It makes it difficult for me. I never seem to fit in, and they
never seem to make much of an effort to include me.*

—RUBIE L.

FIRST-AID KIT

☆ **Give and take.** If you want your mother-in-law to respect you, you must first show her respect. After all, she loved your husband first and raised him to be the man he is today. It's a give-and-take relationship, and you must be willing to give first.

☆ **Make time.** To build a better relationship with your mother-in-law, call her up and ask her out for lunch one day or spend an evening together. Show her that you want to get to know her better, that you desire her company.

☆ **Know when to lead.** Allow your husband to take the lead when any conflict arises with his family, and you take the lead when any conflict arises with yours.

☆ **Respect.** No matter what your relationship with your in-laws is like, you should always treat them with respect. Showing kindness and respect can get you through many tough family holidays.

☆ **Grandparents.** Your parents and your in-laws are very important to your children's well-being. Make time for them to visit with your children, and allow your children to build lasting relationships with them.

☆ **Support.** Don't underestimate the value of the solid support system you have in your in-laws. If you are fortunate enough to live near them, listen to the advice from Grandma and Grandpa. Take advantage of their willingness to baby-sit for you from time to time, making sure to let them know how much you appreciate it.

S.O.S.
(SPIRITUAL OPPORTUNITY TO SAVOR)

Now Elimelech, Naomi's husband, died, and she was left with her two sons. They married Moabite women, one named Orpah and the other Ruth. After they had lived there about ten years, both Mahlon and Kilion also died, and Naomi was left without her two sons and her husband....

Then Naomi said to her two daughters-in-law, "Go back, each of you, to your mother's home. May the LORD show kindness to you, as you have shown to your dead and to me. May the LORD grant that each of you will find rest in the home of another husband."

Then she kissed them and they wept aloud and said to her, "We will go back with you to your people."

But Naomi said, "Return home, my daughters. Why would you come with me? Am I going to have any more sons, who

could become your husbands? Return home, my daughters;
I am too old to have another husband. Even if I thought there
was still hope for me—even if I had a husband tonight and
then gave birth to sons—would you wait until they grew up?
Would you remain unmarried for them? No, my daughters.
It is more bitter for me than for you, because the LORD's hand
has gone out against me!"

   At this they wept again. Then Orpah kissed her mother-in-
law good-by, but Ruth clung to her.
                    RUTH 1:3–5, 8–14

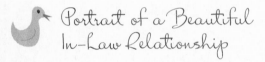
Portrait of a Beautiful In-Law Relationship

One of the best examples of a loving mother-in-law and daughter-in-law relationship is in the biblical story about Ruth and her mother-in-law, Naomi.

When Naomi urged both of her widowed daughters-in-law to return to their own mother's homes, Ruth clung to her and said, "Where you go I will go, and where you stay I will stay. Your people will be my people and your God my God" (Ruth 1:16).

Then Ruth set up home with Naomi, worked to provide food and shelter for Naomi. When Ruth met and married Boaz, she continued to care for Naomi. And when she gave birth to her son, she laid him on Naomi's lap. Talk about reflecting God's love to a mother-in-law!

Ruth represents a lost ideal.[5] Can you imagine leaving your hometown, let alone your home country, to live with and care for your mother-in-law?

When I married Mike, I knew I was also marrying into his family, just as he was marrying into mine. But I'm not sure I was quite prepared for what that meant, especially when it came to having a mother-in-law.

Mike is an only son with three sisters, and throughout his growing-up years, he was very close to his mom. Mike's mom is a lot like me in some ways and very different in others. Finding balance in our relationship has taken years, as well as patience and understanding on both our parts. And though we both make mistakes, ours has grown into a beautiful give-and-take relationship in which we accept, love, and support each other as is.

You don't have to be just like your mother-in-law. You do, however, need to learn to love her for who she is. After all, she raised a little boy into the godly man you chose to marry. What an amazing gift she has given you!

Study Questions

1. What is your relationship with your mother-in-law like? Are you kind to her? Do you respect her?
2. Do you make your mother-in-law feel like part of your family? Or is she more of an outsider?
3. Can you see yourself doing for your mother-in-law what Ruth did for Naomi? Why or why not?
4. Write down three things you can do this month to show your mother-in-law you love her and appreciate her for who she is.

Part 4

Choosing Joy

Gaining Love

The Itsy-Bitsy Spider

The itsy-bitsy spider
Climbed up the water spout;
Down came the rain
And washed the spider out;
Out came the sun
And dried up all the rain;
And the itsy-bitsy spider
Climbed up the spout again.

Reaching the Summit

Finding Humor in the Chaos

Water from the Word

A cheerful look brings joy to the heart.

PROVERBS 15:30

We are not good dancers, Mike and I. But we love to dance as much as our kids do. In fact, the goofier we get, the more fun we all have.

If someone were to peer into our kitchen window on an evening when our dancing is in full swing, they might think we have gone off the deep end. There we would be, arms flailing, wiggling this way and that, looking more like a circus act than dancers.

Mike and I started dancing in the kitchen long before we became parents. The first two years we were married, we were poor as dirt. I was still in graduate school, and Mike's full-time job was delivering furniture. Our typical evening meal was mac 'n' cheese casserole, hot dogs, or whatever we had scavenged from our parents' pantries (with their permission, of course).

That never bothered us much at all. We were so happy. No—scratch that; we were *joyful*. We took pleasure in the simple act of being together in our tiny little apartment. In the dim glow of candlelight, while the dishes soaked in the sink (we were too poor for a dishwasher), we would slow dance to our favorite songs on the radio. As long as we danced together after supper, the day ended on a joyful note.

Dancing to a New Tune

Now that we have kids to keep us busy, we don't enjoy many post-dinner slow dances in the kitchen anymore. These days we fast-dance to *Veggie Rocks,* Chris Rice, or our Bibleman CD. We do have some good nights, and yes, we have some bad nights too. That's life with kids.

On our good nights, after supper is over, one of the kids starts the CD player, and music fills the air. There we are—four kids and two adults, arms flailing, singing at the top of our lungs, and dancing. The faster the song, the better we like it. Our kids love to jump and bounce to the rhythm. Joy fills the air in our kitchen, and it is as sweet as the smell of homemade bread baking in the oven.

Then there are those nights when life drags us down and devours our joy. We carry around stresses from work and home like luggage. The

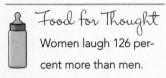

Food for Thought
Women laugh 126 percent more than men. Women tend to do the most laughing, while men tend to do the most laugh-getting.[1]

bills are due, the carpets are a mess, the dishes are dirty, and the kids have homework. Laundry is piled high in the basement, and toys are strewn across the family room floor.

On those nights we probably need to dance in the kitchen more than ever. But we don't. Instead, we pass the grumpies around like the flu, and no one is immune. The downward spiral starts right at the dinner table as we moan and groan about what still needs to be done. As soon as supper is over, the race begins.

I load the washing machine. Laundry in progress? *Check*. Still feeling grumpy.

Next the yelling begins. "Colin! Riley! It's bath time!" It usually takes about four hollers to get them moving. By then, my mood has shifted downward even more, and I feel the blood pulsing in my head.

I march upstairs, each step a resounding thud that echoes through the house. As I pass by the kitchen on my way to grab pajamas for the kids, I notice Mike working on the dinner dishes.

Dishes started? *Check*. Still feeling grumpy.

As Mike loads the dishwasher, he barely looks at me. Well, no time to linger; parenting responsibilities wait for no one.

Hardly looking them in the eyes, I get the two little ones into the bathtub.

Baths in progress? *Check*. Still feeling grumpy.

Next, we nag Hannah until she starts practicing the piano.

Piano practice underway? *Check*.

Where did Sydney go? Doesn't she know she has spelling words to study?

Still feeling grumpy—and now my headache settles in. Although the items on my to-do list are getting done, my mood has not improved. In fact, it is getting worse.

Joyful or Grumpy?

On those kinds of nights, the faster we move, the worse we feel. The more we push the kids, the grumpier they get. The grumpier they become, the grumpier *we* get. It's a vicious cycle of negative emotions that sucks the joy right out of our family.

I've come to realize that my mood isn't directly connected to my to-do list or my stress level. No, my mood is intertwined with my attitude. Getting things done does not improve my attitude.

Those grumpy nights have become fewer and farther between at our home in the last few years, because of one thing: *choice.* We make a decision to be joyful and to have a joyful home.

The key to maintaining a positive attitude lies in the way you look at life. You can determine to be joyful. It is a decision you will have to make every day. Even when things go wrong, you can choose not to let it get you down. If it does, you can still choose not to drag your family down with you.

Murphy's Law Vacations

During 1998, we had the summer of Murphy's Law vacations.

It all started when one-year-old Sydney came down with a double ear infection while our family was at Camp Luther, the family church camp we attend every summer. She recovered only after a trip to the emergency room and a round of antibiotics.

Next was the doomed camping trip. En route to meet Mike's parents at a campsite for the weekend, three-year-old Hannah threw up in the car. After Mike and I finished a monumental cleanup job, Hannah begged that we continue on; against our better judgment, we consented. Soon after setting up camp, we were hit by a monsoon-size rainstorm and everything in our tent got soaked. Then Hannah burned her hand on a lantern. We retreated home that very night to lick our wounds.

Our final family getaway that summer was to a resort for a night of swimming and relaxation. It was actually a fabulous vacation, and the kids had a blast. But on the way home, our car broke down. We were close enough to a repair shop that we coasted into the parking lot, but we had to wait three hours for a ride home.

After the many disasters we had already encountered that summer, you might assume our attitudes were horrible—but they weren't. Instead, while waiting for my sister-in-law to pick us up, we sat in the grassy yard outside the repair shop and played games with the girls. We pulled out our cooler, ate snacks, and sang songs. We made the choice to be joyful, to enjoy the blessing of being together. As a result, we created a wonderful family memory in the midst of a crisis.

How? By maintaining a positive attitude. By remaining joyful along life's bumpy road. By "dancing in the kitchen," so to speak, despite broken-down cars and three-hour waits.

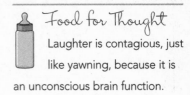

Food for Thought

Laughter is contagious, just like yawning, because it is an unconscious brain function.

But when we talk, we stop laughing, because speech trumps laughter, and we can't do both simultaneously.

So stop talking so much and let yourself laugh at life![2]

The reality is that there will always be bills to pay and work to be done, laundry to be washed, and supper to be cooked. Not everyone will be nice to you, and your kids won't always listen.

Those bumps are a given; they are to be expected. What you *can* change is how you react to them. So on grumpy nights, take joy in little things like dancing in the kitchen. Let your kids lead the way. Find pleasure in simple rituals. Play music and don't be afraid to let loose and dance. Of course, you may want to close the curtains first so no one calls the paramedics!

Good for the Heart

Laughter is good medicine. In fact, research by cardiologists at the University of Maryland indicates that "laughter, along with an active sense of humor, may help protect you against a heart attack." Laughter may also help prevent heart disease. "People with heart disease were 40 percent less likely to laugh in a variety of situations compared to people of the same age without heart disease."[3]

Food for Thought

Laughter is modeled by the mother during the baby's first year of life: The more mom laughs, the more baby laughs.

Between one and four months of age, babies laughed 0.08 times per minute while interacting with their mothers.

At twelve months, babies laughed 0.27 times per minute while interacting with their mothers.

By two years, toddlers laughed 0.30 times per minute (eighteen laughs per hour) while interacting with their mothers.

Moms' laughter rates were stable at 0.55 laughs per minute (thirty-three per hour) while they interacted with their babies or toddlers.[4]

Babies offer an excellent example of unfettered joy. They smile and giggle at the smallest things. Once you get them going, it's like unleashing a clown. They just keep laughing and laughing, and you can't help but giggle right along with them.

Amazingly, research has proven that babies don't teach us to laugh; *we teach them.* As moms interact with their babies—playing, tickling, and giggling—moms show them how to laugh and find joy. Studies have found that the more a mom laughs, the more her baby or toddler will laugh. And the first year is crucial to modeling that behavior. After babies reach two years of age, their laughter rates level off and stabilize.[5]

So what should we do? We need to plan time to laugh with our babies, to let go of our inhibitions. We need to play with them, lay them on the floor, and sit with them as we toss a ball back and forth or tickle their adorable little piggies.

Colin was the happiest baby I've ever seen. He smiled at everyone and laughed at everything. If you cooed at him, he would let loose with a major gigglefest. He was ticklish, especially on his back. We would run our fingers along his spine from top to bottom, and he would giggle and laugh so loud you couldn't help but join in.

That's the best thing about laughter: it's contagious. If someone around you is laughing, even if you don't know why, something deep inside you wants to join in. Laughter is healthy and healing; it is good for the soul. We need to laugh through our days more often than we probably do.

Babies usually laugh for the first time at three or four months. Like Colin's case, the laughter is usually in response to being tickled or some other physical stimulation, according to *Parenting* magazine: "After the six-month mark, they have a better grasp of their tiny world and begin to understand that something unexpected and out of the ordinary can be hilarious."[6] It really isn't complicated. All you have to do is get down on the floor and get silly with your baby.

Letting Go

I think the hardest part of learning to laugh is letting go of our grown-up inhibitions.

Let's face it: none of us wants to look weird; none of us wants to look silly or immature. But we have to act like no one is watching. We have to forget how it looks and let ourselves get silly with our children.

One of my kids' best memories cost me nothing, yet several years later they still talk about it as if it were the greatest event of their lives. It started on a warm spring day while it was raining.

Now, I'm not usually a mom who lets my kids play in the rain—it's too messy. And who ends up doing the muddy laundry? Me. But on this particular day, I thought, *What the heck?*

"Hey, let's go out and play in the rain!" I said. There was no thunder or lightning, and it was plenty warm. So we all headed out to get muddy. The kids swung on their swing set, ran and jumped in mud puddles, and tried to catch raindrops in their mouths. Meanwhile, I brought the camera outside to capture some of those precious moments.

We spent about an hour outside in the rain, getting our clothes and our feet sopping wet. We saw frogs and worms come out to play; we collected sticks and wet leaves just for fun. And through it all, we laughed at one another and at ourselves.

I'm so glad that I let them play in the rain that day. And I'm so glad I took the time to join them in their playing. I let go of my mommy anxieties and worries and just had *fun* with them.

Someday, when I'm old and gray and they have children of their own, I hope my kids will remember the times we spent dancing in the kitchen and playing in the rain. I hope I helped them learn to laugh at life and enjoy the ride.

Faith on Fire

Dear Lord,
You gave me the gift of laughter and the place to find true joy.
Help me remember to choose joy, no matter what my circum-
stances are at the time. Show me the giggles on the inside and
the smiles on the outside, and remind me not to take life too seri-
ously. Life is a gift from You. I want to rejoice in every moment,
to grab each song, and to dance my way through the day.
In Jesus's name,
amen.

Shelter from the Storm

Of course, not every day of motherhood is joyful.
Some are exasperating, and some are days of sheer survival.
But in the long run, it's the most purposeful,
meaningful job I've ever had the privilege of doing.
—BRENDA N.

I can usually feel myself getting grumpy, like a steam pot
getting ready to boil. Sometimes I think about stopping it, but I don't.
Then when I get angry, I don't feel better; I usually feel worse.
—CONNIE V.

Yes, I raise my voice above a whisper. In fact, I yell at my kids.
There, I admitted it. And no, I'm not proud of it. It is something
I'm working on improving each day I'm a mom.
—KARRIE K.

Sometimes when I'm in a bad mood and feel the joy slipping
just out of reach, I put on some great Christian music and jam to it
in the kitchen as I clean up the meal. Usually that does the trick,
and life is back in perspective again.
—JESSIE A.

FIRST-AID KIT

Ten Ways to Laugh with Your Baby

1. Lay your baby on a blanket on the floor and tickle his legs and toes for a second or two. Tease with "Is Mommy getting your piggies?"

2. Make animal noises with your baby. *Moo* like a cow, *baa* like a sheep, *meow* like a cat. Pretend to be the animal you are imitating and see if you can get her to play along.

3. Put a funny hat on your head, or put a hat on backward or upside down. Anything out of the ordinary will get him giggling.

4. Play peekaboo with your baby by putting your hands over your eyes or by "hiding behind" a small towel or blanket. When you reveal your face, make a different expression each time.

5. Get out your old pots and pans and a few wooden spoons, and make your own band. You start hitting the pans, then let your baby have a turn. Between songs, be sure to laugh with her.

6. Put a silly song on the radio and dance with your baby. Swing him around to the rhythm of the song, dip him low, and sing out loud.

7. Do something unexpected, like letting your baby eat a cookie right there on the kitchen floor. Let her make a complete mess, and be sure to join her in the fun.

8. Play hide-and-seek baby-style by crawling on the floor and hiding behind a chair or a corner. Peek out, then duck back. Your baby is sure to laugh.

9. Have a crawling race with your baby on the floor. Get down on your hands and knees and crawl wherever he does. Imitate his every move and see how long it takes for him to laugh.

10. Play Simon says by mimicking your baby's hand movements. Match her like a mirror and see if she notices. When she does, see if you can get her to mimic yours.

S.O.S.
(SPIRITUAL OPPORTUNITY TO SAVOR)

As Jesus started on his way, a man ran up to him and fell on his knees before him. "Good teacher," he asked, "what must I do to inherit eternal life?"

"Why do you call me good?" Jesus answered. "No one is good—except God alone. You know the commandments: 'Do not murder, do not commit adultery, do not steal, do not give false testimony, do not defraud, honor your father and mother.'"

"Teacher," he declared, "all these I have kept since I was a boy."

Jesus looked at him and loved him. "One thing you lack," he said. "Go, sell everything you have and give to the poor, and you will have treasure in heaven. Then come, follow me."

At this the man's face fell. He went away sad, because he had great wealth.

MARK 10:17–22

 ## Happily Ever After

I believed in happily ever after when I was a little girl. After all, Cinderella, Snow White, and Sleeping Beauty all found their Prince Charming and rode off into the sunset to live happily ever after, right?

But that is where their story ended. The credits rolled; the movie was done. What do you think happened next? Did Cinderella like becoming a princess? Did she get along with the king and queen? Did Snow White stay in touch with the Seven Dwarfs? Did Sleeping Beauty ever forgive the Evil Queen for feeding her that apple?

Those are fairy tales, and their story ends where ours begins. When we say "I do," it is a beginning, not an ending. There is no sunset to ride off into, no happily ever after. Every day we get to decide how to live life. We must make the conscious choice to be joyful no matter what our circumstances.

What Jesus asked of the rich young man in the gospel of Mark was complete devotion—to sell all he had and come follow Him. For that, Jesus promised him treasure in heaven. But the rich man was so attached to his earthly possessions that instead of following Jesus, he simply walked away. He chose sadness.

What will you choose? Will you choose to follow Jesus in all you do? Or will you hold on to the little things and walk away sad?

Study Questions

1. What in your life is making you sad? stressed out?
2. Do you let the daily chaos of life get you down?
3. How do you feel when you are having a good day, when everything goes your way?
4. Do you let your sadness impact your mothering? How?
5. Try this breathing exercise next time you feel sad or stressed out: Inhale and exhale ten deep breaths, counting to ten on the way in and on the way out. Then ask God to help you be joyful no matter what your day is like. If *that* doesn't work, go hug your baby!

Camouflaging Your Imperfections

Becoming the Mom You Want to Be

Water from the Word

God is love. Whoever lives in love lives in God,
and God in him.

1 JOHN 4:16

Guilty! Confession time.

Sometimes I like to sleep late, as in 10 a.m. or later. (Of course I rarely get the chance anymore.)

Sometimes I'm a grump in the morning. After a late night of laundry or writing, I gripe at my kids about not getting ready quickly and lose my cool over the tiniest details.

Sometimes, in order to buy myself thirty minutes of peace and quiet, I occupy my preschooler with a computer game after getting my older kids on the school bus. During those precious moments to myself, I relax on the couch, sip my coffee, and laugh aloud at the first half of *Live with Regis and Kelly.*

Sometimes I hide out in the bathroom. I pretend I'm going potty and lock the door just to have a few minutes to myself without someone tugging on my sleeve, whining, or spilling milk on my pants. Like Sherlock Holmes, they eventually sniff me out.

Sometimes I don't like being a mom: when I'm getting stepped on, spit up on, bitten, or drained of every ounce of energy. In those moments, I don't even want my kids to touch me; it makes my skin crawl. That's usually when I resort to hiding out in the bathroom.

Sometimes I hurt my kids' feelings. I have pretended to listen to their stories; I have skipped pages in the book I'm reading to them at bedtime. Of course, this works only until they hit kindergarten.

And sometimes, when I'm exhausted and their bedtime prayers seem to drone on and on, I have even cut them short by announcing, "No more stories. No more talking. Go to sleep. Mom is *off duty.* I am going downstairs to collapse. So if you value your life, don't—I repeat, *don't*—come down to see me unless you are either bleeding to death or have broken a bone!"

The point of these confessions is that even though I love my children more than life itself, I make mistakes daily. I'm not perfect. I know I don't always meet their needs, and I'm not always the mother God wants me to be. But I *am* the one God chose for my kids, and I have to find the grace in that and trust His decision—even when I question it myself.

Mom Equals Love

Before I became a mom, I thought motherhood would make me more loving, more tender-hearted. I imagined that I would somehow magically transform into the perfect mother, all patience and wisdom. I would always use kind words when I spoke, always have my kids' best interests at heart, always put my needs at the bottom of the list and joyfully meet theirs each moment.

The punch line, of course, is that I didn't change at all. I came into this mothering gig the same person I was before my first baby was born. Impatient. A bit of a control freak. Not liking surprises. Having a temper.

As I travel this path of motherhood, I realize that most of us moms have certain things in common: We aren't the moms we *want* to be. We judge ourselves constantly, and we always fall short. We think that every mom out there is better at it than we are—more patient, more loving, more tender (thinner and prettier too).

The Five Mommy Truths

I've spent a lot of time over the last decade thinking about the kind of mom I want to be. Additionally, I have asked moms all over the country—some in live audiences, some via e-mail—how they feel about their mothering skills. I've reached the conclusion that there are five basic mommy truths you need to know.

Mommy Truth No. 1: *You will not always like your child.*
Now, don't freak out on me here. I know you love your children. I love mine too! But it was a shocker to realize that I won't always *like* them.

When Hannah was a baby, I was your typical overprotective, over-reacting first-time mom. When she cried, I picked her up. When she needed me, I was right there. I hardly let her out of my sight, and I was physically and emotionally drained most of the time.

As I mentioned before, Hannah wasn't a good sleeper—probably because I never gave her an opportunity to develop sleeping skills on her own. But when she was six months old, I decided to introduce a regular napping schedule so I could have a more predictable day. So at 10 a.m. and at 2 p.m., I would place Hannah in her crib for a nap.

Food for Thought

SIX HEALTHY WAYS TO HANDLE ANGER TOWARD YOUR BABY

1. Stop; don't do anything. Never pick up your baby when you are angry.

2. Take ten deep breaths, exhaling slowly each time.

3. If your baby is older than three months, healthy, and your pediatrician has okayed it, then put your baby in a safe place (like his crib) and walk away. Crying won't hurt him.

4. Realize that you need help. Call your mom or a girlfriend and ask her to come over as soon as possible.

5. Get more rest. If you need to hire a baby-sitter so you can grab a few hours of sleep each day, do it.

6. Say positive things to others about your baby. Mention what you love most about her and about being a mom.

Beep! Beep! Beep!

Reality check: Babies don't always do what you want them to do when you want them to do it. No doubt about it, Hannah didn't like my schedule. She declared war on my napping routine and on my sanity as well.

Of course, I did my part to get her ready. I would nurse her, change her diaper, and snuggle and rock her. Then, once she was sound asleep, I would tuck her into her crib and tiptoe downstairs to collapse on the couch.

Beep! Beep! Beep!

Just as I would fall into a deep, restful sleep—the kind in which you forget where you are and maybe even drool on the pillow—Hannah would wake up screaming. Not crying, mind you; *screaming.* At the top of her little girl lungs.

I would awaken, stumble to my feet, and tread heavily upstairs to calm her and try to get her back to sleep. I would nurse her again (big mistake, by the way) and, once she was snoozing, lay her down in her crib. Then I would literally fall down the stairs and head for the couch.

The moment my head hit the pillow, my eyes would close and my muscles would relax. Ah, sleep. Wonderful sleep.

Beep! Beep! Beep!

Again I would be jolted awake by a screaming Hannah. This time my head would be pounding and my vision was blurred. Upstairs I would go, and we would run through our little routine all over again.

Suddenly one day I realized I was angry with Hannah. No, scratch that—I *hated* Hannah. She kept me awake all night long, and then had the audacity not to let me nap during the day! It was a nightmare, and I was losing patience. I also felt like I was losing my mind. That was when I asked my parents and my mother-in-law to each come over once a week to be with Hannah so I could sleep. As long as I took a solid nap several days a week, the other days went better. If I was *really* desperate for rest, I simply napped in the recliner with Hannah lying on top of me.

The biggest surprise for me, as a new mom, was that this precious little baby, this gorgeous tiny girl, could look so horrid to me in those moments. Though I never stopped loving her, not even for one minute, there were moments when I stopped *liking* her. Even more surprising was the fact that once I had a nap, she looked adorable again.

New moms need to realize something important: *there will be times when you don't like your baby.* This may be because he isn't allowing you to sleep, is causing you pain, or is making life miserable. Don't feel guilty; just seek help.

Remember that crying will not hurt a healthy baby, but *you* could hurt your baby in a moment of exhaustion and rage when you aren't thinking straight. If you are at your wit's end, put your baby in a safe place, like in his crib or playpen, and walk away for a few minutes. Shut the door, go into another room, and call your mom or a girlfriend. Tell them you need a break from motherhood, even for just one hour.

Believe me, we have all been there. Any mom who has survived her own baby's first year will completely understand.

Mommy Truth No. 2: Sometimes there are more questions than answers.

I have read so many books on motherhood it makes my head spin. And every book, it seems, claimed to have the answers to all my baby woes: Put her on a feeding schedule. Feed him on demand. Let your baby cry it out. Work at your baby's sleep routine. Breast is best. Bottle-feeding involves your husband. Never use store-bought baby food. Buy organic baby food. Use cloth diapers. Use disposable ones.

Every book I read contained grains of truth, but they all seemed to forget that each mom and each baby have unique personalities, unique lifestyles, and unique needs that can only be met by doing what works for *them*.

I tried a feeding schedule and it failed, so I ended up nursing my babies on demand. I never let Hannah cry herself to sleep, but I let Sydney cry it out at eight months old. Colin slept through the night on his own. I spent the first three months of Riley's life sleeping with her on my stomach in a recliner just so I could get some consistent shuteye.

I may not have done it all the right way, but I did what worked with each of my babies. I did what I could live with at the time. In other words, I strongly believe that there is no perfect way to do anything. Look at your options, talk to your pediatrician, ask other moms what worked for them, and then go by trial and error. In short, you have to do what works for you and for your baby—don't feel guilty that you aren't following some prescribed method in a book.

Mommy Truth No. 3: No mom is perfect.

I'm a people watcher. I love sitting in restaurants or malls and watching people pass by me as I guess their life story.

But when I see another mother, I often make comparisons. She is prettier than I am. She dresses better than I do. She is thinner than I am. Her kids behave better than mine do. She has it all together, while I'm a complete mess.

The more moms I meet, the more I realize that we are all drowning in mommy insecurities, comparing ourselves to one another and believing that every other mom out there knows what she is doing and that she is doing it better than we are.

News flash: *no mom knows what she is doing all of the time.* There, I said it. If your secret is out, I'm sorry.

We need to drop the facade. We spend way too much energy pretending that we're happy all the time, that nursing is going great, that our baby is precious and perfect, and that he never cries or pees on the ceiling. We try to look our best, act our best, and pretend that we do in fact have it all together. We get so good at faking it that we forget it isn't true.

I'm here to tell you that the best gift you can give your girlfriends is being real with them. Invite them over, and don't run your sweeper beforehand. Hang out with them in your sweatpants and no makeup. And get real about motherhood. Don't pretend all is well when it isn't. Tell them about your struggles. You might be surprised when they chime in with "Me too!"

Mommy Truth No. 4: You can't do it alone.

I'm a very independent person, and it took me years to realize that it's okay to ask for help. But motherhood is hands down the toughest job I've ever had. I *can't* do it on my own—nor should I try.

For one thing, my baby has a father who is my partner in this parenting thing. But men are men, and they can't read our minds. Sure, it would be nice if they came home from work and said, "Honey, you look exhausted. You must have had a hard day. Why don't I take the baby for a walk in the stroller while you take a hot shower or a nap?" Okay, reality check! Most men aren't terribly observant or intuitive. The typical exchange sounds more like this:

> Dad: "Hi! I'm home!"
> Mom: "Why are you so late? I expected you an hour ago.
> I have no idea what to make for dinner, Junior is wearing the last diaper in the house, and the washer just broke down." [Mom then shoves Junior into Dad's arms and storms out of the room to make dinner.]
> Dad (sarcastically): "Well, maybe I'll go back to work. At least they were nice to me there."
> Mom (from the kitchen): "Fine! Go back. We'll do just fine without you. We always do!"

Yikes! What a way to begin an evening at home.

Dads want to help. They want to spend time with their children. But they also want to be respected and appreciated. If you choose to show your husband love and honor, you are more likely to have the outcome and the help you desire. New scenario:

> Dad: "Hi, I'm home!"
> Mom: "Hi, honey. How was your day?"
> Dad: "Tough. I had a new case and two committee meetings that went overtime. I'm sorry I'm late. How was your day?"

Mom: "Tough too. I sure could use a little break. Do you
    think you could take Junior for a quick stroller ride
    so I could grab a shower before dinner?"

Dad: "Sure. Just let me change my clothes. Do you want
    me to walk to the corner and pick up a pizza?"

Mom: "That'd be great. I'm so glad you're home. I need
    your help so much."

I know some of you might be gagging at this syrupy dialogue, but
you get my drift. Our husbands want to help, but we have to ask them.
So be direct. Be specific. Don't say, "I need help." He will have no idea
how to help you. Instead, say, "Could you change the baby's diaper
while I start supper?" or "Could you watch him while I go for a walk
around the block?" The more specific you can be, the better.

And remember: Always be kind, respectful, and honest. Ask for
help in the right way, and you will get the help you need.

Mommy Truth No. 5: You will make mistakes.

Before I became a mom, I had no idea the number of mothering mistakes I would make.

Every time I make a mistake, I suffer "mommy guilt." Thank good-
ness the older and more experienced I grow at mothering, the more I
realize that every mom makes mistakes. And that our children are
tougher than we think.

When I do make a mistake, I take the time to apologize to my children, ask for their forgiveness, and pray with them for God's guidance.
In those tender moments, as they realize that Mom makes mistakes and
needs forgiveness, I see true love and compassion in my children's eyes.
I harness these teachable moments, and my children are stronger
because of my honesty.

The first time I made a mom mistake, though, I was devastated. Hannah was about three weeks old and not yet rolling over. We were upstairs in my bedroom, and I needed to run downstairs to grab a clean diaper. So I placed her in the center of our queen bed, put a pillow on either side of her, and ran for the diaper.

As I was heading back, I heard a thump. My heart nearly stopped. I thought I had killed my baby!

I ran up those stairs faster than I ever thought I could and found Hannah on the floor, crying. Apparently she had kicked her legs so hard that she scooted right off the end of the bed, hit the dresser, then fell to the ground.

 *Food for Thought*

COMMON SAFETY MISTAKES EVEN GOOD MOMS MAKE

1. **Risky ride.** Never ride an escalator with a stroller; always take the time to look for an elevator, even if it's a hassle.

2. **Off-balance.** Always place your baby carrier on a low surface within arm's reach and never on a countertop.

3. **Wide reach.** Childproof your home—every room:
   a. Get down on your hands and knees.
   b. Remove items that are within reach.
   c. Check the carpet for buried items.
   d. Keep poisons locked away.
   e. Leave the toll-free number for the Poison Control Center (1-800-222-1222) by your phone.

4. **Hazardous waste.** Before you discard anything in a reachable trash can, consider whether it will be dangerous. Things like razors or cleaning products should be disposed of outside the home.

5. **Watch the step.** Put gates at the top and bottom of your staircase.

6. **Car trouble.** Never leave your child alone in a car, even for a moment.[1]

I grabbed her up, held her, and started crying right along with her. Then I called my pediatrician. (I would have called the National Guard if I thought they would come to help her.)

He settled me down on the phone and asked a few questions. Once I calmed down, I realized that Hannah wasn't hurt at all. No bruises, no bumps, no scratches. I nursed her and she fell asleep. It took me hours, on the other hand, to calm *myself* down. What kind of mom lets her newborn fall off a bed?

Well, I've made plenty more mistakes over the past decade. For instance, Hannah once fell off the porch while chasing a cat. Colin walked out of a restaurant and almost got hit by a car. I was standing six inches from Riley when she fell into my friend's pool—twice! My kids have been bumped and bruised, and sometimes I wonder how they have survived all my mothering mistakes. But somehow they have.

And each time I feel as if I could have done better, I learn something about myself and about my children. I learn not only to ask God for forgiveness; I also learn to forgive myself.

Faith on Fire

Dear Lord,
You are love, and I could never live up to being as loving as You are all the time. But I want to live in love and in You. Please help me be the mom my baby needs, the mom You want me to be. I know I will make mistakes along the way; I ask You to forgive me and help me become a stronger, more faithful mom. Help me not to strive for perfection, since no mom is perfect. Help me to seek Your will, turn to You, and point my children to You through every up and down on my mothering journey. In Jesus's name,
amen.

Shelter from the Storm

*I make a lot of mommy mistakes, but I know it is a
learning process. I'm just thankful to be learning as I go.*
—GEORGIA A.

*Realize that you don't have to have all the answers.
Just make sure you personally know the One who does.*
—ERIN S.

*I will never forget the day I left my newborn in the car by mistake.
It was winter, and I got out to run into the store very quickly.
I got to the front of the store, and panic hit. I ran back to the car
as fast as I could, and I sat in the front seat and cried. In that moment,
I failed as a mom. I just thank God she was okay.*
—DEBBIE L.

*When my firstborn was still a baby, I cut her toenails with
regular-sized clippers. I thought it'd be okay. I ended up accidentally
cutting off some of her toe as well, and she bled for almost
thirty minutes. All because I was in a rush to get it done.*
—MELISSA J.

FIRST-AID KIT

Seven Keys to Becoming the Mom You Want to Be

1. **Forgive.** When you do make a mistake, ask your husband
   and your children to forgive you. Share your heart with
   them, open yourself up, and try harder next time.

2. **Forget.** Try to forget about the mommy mistakes in your past. They are over and done with. You can't go back and change them, so stop stressing about them.

3. **Friends.** Find several girlfriends you can be open and honest with about your mothering. Share your biggest fears and your worst mistakes. Ask for their help when you have hit your kid limit, and be available to help them when they're at their wit's end.

4. **Faith.** Follow Christ's example and find peace in the Lord. Know that you will never be a perfect mom, but you can be the mom God wants you to be if you lean on Him and seek His will for your mothering.

5. **Frame.** Frame your life with love, family, and friends who love you and your family.

6. **Follow.** Choose a mentor mom. Find an older and more experienced mom who is willing to nurture and teach you.

7. **Fair.** Be fair to yourself. At least once a week take a time-out from mothering. Get away from your baby even if it's just to the grocery store.

S.O.S.
(SPIRITUAL OPPORTUNITY TO SAVOR)

Every year [Jesus's] parents went to Jerusalem for the Feast of the Passover. When he was twelve years old, they went up to the Feast, according to the custom. After the Feast was over, while his parents were returning home, the boy Jesus stayed behind in Jerusalem, but they were unaware of it. Thinking he was in their company, they traveled on for a day. Then they began looking for him among their relatives and friends. When they did not find him, they went back to Jerusalem to look for him. After three days they found him in the temple courts, sitting among the teachers, listening to them and asking them questions. Everyone who heard him was amazed at his understanding and his answers. When his parents saw him, they were astonished. His mother said to him, "Son, why have you treated us like this? Your father and I have been anxiously searching for you."

"Why were you searching for me?" he asked. "Didn't you know I had to be in my Father's house?" But they did not understand what he was saying to them.

Then he went down to Nazareth with them and was obedient to them. But his mother treasured all these things in her heart. And Jesus grew in wisdom and stature, and in favor with God and men.

LUKE 2:41–52

 Parenting Mistakes 101

Before I was a mom, I thought I had it all figured out. I even used to feel the need to judge moms I would see out in the mall or at restaurants. I would see their mistakes and whisper in a know-it-all voice to whoever would listen, "Do you *believe* they are letting those kids do that?" or "When we have kids, they will behave better than that!"

Well, let me tell you that there's nothing more annoying than a know-it-all who hasn't lived it all. And without being a mom myself, I had no business judging any mom who was doing her best to make it through until bedtime.

I could list all the mommy mistakes I've made over the last dozen years, but it would probably bore you to death (and besides, there probably isn't room in this book). Instead, I want to talk about what to do *when* you make a mistake.

When your children are babies, they won't understand that you made a mistake. But you can still apologize to them, pray about it, and ask God to help you do better next time.

As your children grow, your life becomes more complex and your mistakes can get even bigger. But I have learned over the years that my kids already know I am not perfect, so why pretend? Even Mary and Joseph lost Jesus once. Boy, I'll bet they felt terrible! Can you imagine the guilt they carried? So when I make a mom-size mistake—when I yell, scream, or lose my temper, when I take out my frustration on one of my kids—I apologize. I sit down with the child, look him or her straight in the eye, and say, "I am so sorry that I lost my temper with you today. I hope you can forgive me and know that I will do my best not to do that again."

I also pray, right there in front of my child, for God's forgiveness and His help to be the mom He wants me to be. The mom my kids need me to be.

The result is that I see in my children's eyes not only forgiveness, but love. They get it. After all, they are human too. We all are in need of God's grace.

Study Questions

1. What mommy mistakes have you made? Were they big ones or little ones?

2. Did you ask for God's forgiveness? Did you forgive yourself?

3. How do you react when your kids make a mistake? What about when your husband makes a mistake?

4. How can you use your mistakes as teachable moments for your kids as they grow and mature?

Discovering Camp Palooza

Finding Fun in the Everyday

Water from the Word

Rejoice and be glad, because great is your reward in heaven.

MATTHEW 5:12

Palooza (n.): Something outstanding of its kind.[1]

There is a place where the sunsets are golden orange, where the days seem to last forever, and where the fun never ends. It is a place where songs are sung, hot dogs are roasted over open fires, and dessert consists of marshmallows, graham crackers, and Hershey bars. A place where the sizzle of summer heat brings out sprinklers, hoses, and kiddy pools.

It's called Camp Palooza, and it's just around the corner. Summertime is perfect Camp Palooza weather (and this coming from a woman who prefers air conditioning from June through the end of August!).

Yes, Ohio summers are very hot, sometimes even sweltering. No, we don't have a backyard in-ground pool. What makes summertime so special for us is the slower pace and emptier calendars. It is the gift of time. Time spent with our kids.

I have not always appreciated that gift of time. Summers sometimes meant rushing around and sweating all the while. But kids have a way of bringing out the best in you, if you only let them. So I did.

Kids have a way of teaching us to appreciate the little things in life. Let yourself catch the spirit they bring to the world, the excitement they embrace in everyday things like summer. With a little encouragement, kids can take you on the ride of your life, with adventures around every twist and turn.

They can turn an ordinary summer into Camp Palooza.

Food for Thought

WHAT'S YOUR BABY'S PLAY PERSONALITY?

The Joker finds humor in all aspects of life.

The World Explorer is curious about the world and loves to go on adventures.

The Physical Explorer is a wilderness traveler, climber, skier, base jumper, scuba diver.

The Intellectual Explorer uncovers the frontiers of science, computer technology, medicine, literature, art, philosophy, psychology.

The Competitor plays to win, regardless of the game. Can be an athlete, entrepreneur, video gamer, stock market player.

The Artist finds beauty in any form, creates art, designs buildings or clothes, writes.

The Director runs the whole show. Some direct films; others direct countries.

The Storyteller creates worlds of imagination for the enjoyment of others.

The Collector is one who collects for fun and sometimes for profit.

The Performer puts on a show for others. Includes actors, models, musicians.

The Craftsman: loves to make things. Includes cooking, carpentry, quilting, model building, sewing, fly tying.[2]

A Camping State of Mind

Our family started the Camp Palooza tradition in the summer of 2003.

It began as a simple idea. Before school let out for summer vacation, we sat down with our four kids (then ages eight, six, four, and one) to plan our summer activities. We asked them to list everything they wanted to do over summer vacation. The list was very long. But we were amazed at the simple nature of many of their choices.

Their lists included weenie roasts, hayrides, zoo trips, and swimming in Lake Erie. Simpler activities, too, like running through the sprinklers, having a picnic supper, or going to the local park.

We made a final copy of our Camp Palooza list and hung it on the bulletin board in our kitchen. As the summer heat sizzled, we started to work our way down the list, checking off each activity as we accomplished it. The kids even started some mornings by running to the bulletin board to see what activities we might get to do that day. Every day was an adventure waiting to happen.

The most amazing thing we have learned from Camp Palooza is that even when things don't go our way, we still have a blast. When I think about that summer and how much fun we had doing everything on our list, the name Camp Palooza fits like a glove. Turns out Camp Palooza isn't about our list of summer adventures, it is about accomplishing something outstanding with our family. It's about making the choice to simply have fun with our kids.

One day during Camp Palooza 2003, we packed a picnic lunch (to cut down on the cost) and headed north to the Cleveland Metroparks Zoo for a fun-filled day of elephant and zebra watching. We spent the morning walking in the sunshine through the maze of exhibits.

About two hours into our expedition, it started to rain. My initial inclination was to pack up and head for home. Then I saw the looks on my kids' faces. They loved it! They weren't frowning or running for cover. Instead, the cool rain provided a welcome relief from the summer heat. Pretty soon they were jumping in the puddles and singing with joy.

So we let them lead the way, and we just followed. I stopped worrying about everything getting wet and began to enjoy the adventure. We ended up spending the rest of the afternoon kicking rain puddles, getting wetter than the hippo in the pond. What could have been a disappointing, failed field trip turned into a wonderful family memory.

What made the difference? Letting go of our expectations and accepting the gift of time. That's exactly what makes Camp Palooza so special. It doesn't have to be perfect; you just need to enjoy being together.

So don't sweat the small stuff. For example, if you lack an outdoor campfire for roasting hot dogs or making s'mores, prepare them in the microwave. No tent? Throw a blanket over a picnic table. If there is snow on the ground, build a snowman. You might just discover Camp Palooza works for any season.

 Food for Thought

Even before babies can walk and talk, their brains are developing.

Neural pathways are the connections that allow information to travel through the brain.

The more pathways, the larger the brain.

Interestingly, the neural pathways that are developed in your child's first three years act like road maps to later learning.

A child with a larger brain (more neural pathways) may learn more easily once she gets into school.

One study from Baylor College of Medicine indicated that babies who are given the opportunity to play often and who are held and touched often as infants have larger brains with more neural pathways.[3]

Spotlights and Tantrums

For me, it was tough staying active and having fun when Hannah was a baby. I was so nervous that I opted to stay home more than I should have.

By the time our second and third babies came along, I learned to drag them along to wherever we were going. However, it isn't always easy to take babies out and about. Sometimes I end up heading for home long before I plan to.

I'll never forget one of those mom moments when I looked more like a circus act than a mom. I packed the diaper bags and carted my toddler (Hannah) and baby (Sydney) off to a football game to watch Mike coach. By the second quarter, Sydney had clearly hit her football limit. She was fussing, crying, and arching her back. I knew she needed to go to bed. But convincing Hannah to leave before halftime was like trying to talk a lion out of the steak in its mouth. So I planted one babe on each hip and just left the game.

As I made my way out of the football stands, I felt like a giant spotlight was aimed directly at me. On my one hip, Hannah was screaming at the top of her lungs and wriggling to break free of my grasp; on the other, Sydney was throwing her head back so hard, I thought I might drop her. As we wove our way through the crowd and out to the parking lot, their tantrums escalated. That was when Hannah decided to throw herself on the grass.

There I was, with a split-second decision to make. I couldn't carry both Sydney and Hannah to the car, at least not with Hannah in the midst of her outburst and Sydney throwing herself around like an angry acrobat. So I left Hannah sitting in the grass between two vehicles while I ran to our car as fast as I could. This motion bounced Sydney up and down and made her cry even louder. I placed Sydney in her car seat, buckled her in, and ran back to retrieve Hannah.

I was so thankful Hannah hadn't decided to return to the football game—or worse—run onto the pavement and been hit by a car. It wasn't a shining mom moment, but it was a mom moment nonetheless. I think I skipped the next football game and put the girls to bed early. But my hiatus from the real world didn't last forever. Before long, I was out there again, baby on one hip, toddler on the other, trying to live a normal life and find fun in the everyday.

Of course you don't have to attend high-school football games to keep your baby active. (However, watching her bounce and dance while the marching band plays is a hoot and a half.) Keeping your baby active can be as easy as playing with him wherever you are.

Food for Thought

MAKING THE MOST OF THE BRAIN GAIN

By the age of five, children's brains are at 90 percent of their potential.[4]

Hold and touch your baby often. Talk and sing to your baby. Every kind of physical activity with babies is important to their overall development.

Every movement encourages brain activity, which, in turn, plays a role in cognitive, emotional, and social development.

Infants should be exposed to new environments, such as exploring different rooms, going outside, taking a stroll, and seeing what other children or people are doing.

Infants should be allowed to move as much as possible. They should spend as little time as necessary in car seats, strollers, playpens, or anything else that keeps them from stretching their legs, kicking, rolling over, and so on.[5]

Respond to your baby. When your baby cries or coos, he is trying to get your attention. Responding builds trust.

Offer your baby the gift of consistency. A home with reliable, consistent, loving care helps build trust and a sense of security in babies that promotes healthy emotions.

For example, babies love to bang pots and pans together. They love exploring new rooms. They love crawling in the backyard. And they love being around other babies.

When you make time to hold your baby, coo at him, respond to his noises or words, or interact with him in any other way, his brain makes thousands of important learning connections. My advice is not to waste time with *Baby Einstein* videos. There's nothing wrong with them, but what your baby needs most is *you.* Just you.

It really is that simple.

Faith on Fire

Dear Lord,

Thank You for the gift of joy and fun, for wanting us to enjoy life. I know that I sometimes feel bogged down by motherhood and trapped indoors with my baby. Help me take that first step and get out and enjoy life. Remind me to find fun in the simple things and to see the world through the eyes of my baby as he explores the world around him. Thank You for my precious baby and his curious mind. Remind me to make the time to simply hold and love him, talk to him, and touch him with Your love.

In Jesus's name,

amen.

Shelter from the Storm

Even when we were pinching pennies in graduate school, we found fun things to do. We looked forward to daily walks with our neighbors, free library story times, and play groups. At least

three times a week, I tried to plan something that involved getting out
of the house for a little bit—even if it was only a walk down the street.

—HEATHER I.

As moms, we say no so often that sometimes it's just great
fun to say yes. When my son was a toddler and our family was
eating out at a restaurant, I surprised him and ordered a dessert
as a treat. The look on his face was the best! Surprising your
kids isn't just fun; it keeps them on their toes—they can't
quite figure you out. That's to a mom's advantage!

—LISA G.

My baby's favorite thing was hanging out in the backyard.
I would stretch out a blanket and lay him on it, and he would
look at the clouds and the trees and just take it all in.

—JENNY P.

Some girlfriends and I started a play group so our babies
would have playtime with other children. We get together twice a month.
The first time is with our children at someone's house, and the host
provides lunch for all. The second time is in the evening
without the kids, so just us moms can have one kid-free night out
each month to share conversation and laughter.

—KATHY T.

Playing with your baby is really as simple as 1-2-3:
(1) Get out some pots and pans and wooden spoons,
(2) get down on the floor with your baby, and
(3) make as much noise as possible and laugh out loud.

—COURTNEY F.

FIRST-AID KIT

- **Nature hike.** Pack your baby in the stroller or backpack and take her out on a community trail. She will enjoy looking at the trees and listening to the birds. Your older kids can collect leaves and acorns for creating a nature design on a poster board.

- **Story time.** Many local libraries offer free story times for babies and toddlers. It helps babies and moms socialize.

- **Backyard banter.** Kids of all ages, especially babies, love to spend time outside. Take your baby to the backyard and lay him on a blanket. Play with him, look at the clouds, and if he can crawl or walk, let him go exploring back there. Older siblings can have a scavenger hunt by collecting bugs, pine cones, leaves, and rocks while you play with the baby.

- **Waterworks.** Fill your bathtub or kiddy pool outside with two inches of warm water, and let your baby sit and play with some toys. She will love to splash and get you wet, and especially love not having to get her hair washed. (Note: Never leave babies unattended in or near water, as they can drown in mere inches.)

- **Free summer concerts.** Many communities sponsor free outdoor concerts in the summer at local parks. Pack a picnic and make an evening of it with your baby. You'll be amazed at how much he loves to bounce and wiggle to the music.

- **Outdoor Olympics.** Create your own family summer Olympics by building a baby obstacle course with soft baby toys, large pillows, and big balls. See if you can get baby to crawl or walk through the obstacle course with you.

- **Free swimming.** Many city pools offer free admission in the evenings, usually an hour before closing. Check it out and get ready for some pool time fun with your baby.

- **Playground reviews.** Check out the playgrounds in and around your community. While you let your baby play, have the older children review and rank their favorites, so you know where to go next time.
- **Night hike.** After dark, take your baby outside for a night hike in the backyard. Look up at the stars, catch lightning bugs, and help her observe the world around her.
- **Picnic dinner.** Have a picnic in your backyard. Spread out a blanket and bring your supper outside. Let your baby eat, then play on the swing set. For dessert, surprise him with ice cream cones or popsicles. And if it's too cold or raining outside, throw a picnic inside on the family room floor.

S.O.S.
(SPIRITUAL OPPORTUNITY TO SAVOR)

Ezra the scribe stood on a high wooden platform built for the occasion. Beside him on his right stood Mattithiah, Shema, Anaiah, Uriah, Hilkiah and Maaseiah; and on his left were Pedaiah, Mishael, Malkijah, Hashum, Hashbaddanah, Zechariah and Meshullam.

Ezra opened the book. All the people could see him because he was standing above them; and as he opened it, the people all stood up. Ezra praised the LORD, the great God; and all the people lifted their hands and responded, "Amen! Amen!" Then they bowed down and worshiped the LORD with their faces to the ground.

The Levites—Jeshua, Bani, Sherebiah, Jamin, Akkub, Shabbethai, Hodiah, Maaseiah, Kelita, Azariah, Jozabad, Hanan and Pelaiah—instructed the people in the Law while

the people were standing there. They read from the Book of the
Law of God, making it clear and giving the meaning so that
the people could understand what was being read.

Then Nehemiah the governor, Ezra the priest and scribe,
and the Levites who were instructing the people said to them
all, "This day is sacred to the LORD your God. Do not mourn
or weep." For all the people had been weeping as they listened
to the words of the Law.

Nehemiah said, "Go and enjoy choice food and sweet
drinks, and send some to those who have nothing prepared.
This day is sacred to our Lord. Do not grieve, for the joy of the
LORD is your strength."

NEHEMIAH 8:4–10

 ## Life Lessons from Ma Ma Hart

Both of my grandfathers died when I was fairly young, and my Grandma
Cipollone died when I was in junior high. I grew closer to my maternal
grandma, Grandma Knoedler, when she came to live with us after she
was diagnosed with cancer. She died when I was a senior in high school,
and I was the one holding her hand when she took her final breath.

When I met Mike, I was truly grandparentless. Then we got married, and my family grew. That was when Ma Ma Hart became my
grandma.

Ellen Brillhart is grandma to the world. She is Mike's maternal
grandma, and she turned ninety-one in 2007. She loves to play euchre,
marbles, and just about any other game you can talk her into. When she
comes over for dinner, she always insists on helping me fold laundry and
especially loves sorting my socks.

From the time Hannah was born, Ellen was Ma Ma Hart to us.

Though she has taught me many life lessons and helped me grow deeper in my faith, the biggest thing I've learned from Ma Ma Hart is to enjoy each day, each moment I am given, for it just might be my last.

Her favorite song is "This is the day that the Lord has made, we will rejoice and be glad in it." When you tell her, "I'll see you Friday evening," she always responds with, "Lord willing, I'll be there."

Like me, she grew up as a city girl and married into this farm life. She has thirty-two great-grandchildren and counting, and she can name every one of them if you ask her to.

Sometimes, as busy moms, we take our walk with the Lord so seriously that we forget how much God wants us to enjoy the life He gave us. "Go and enjoy choice food and sweet drinks…for the joy of the LORD is your strength." Yes, the joy of the Lord should be our strength each day.

My Grandma Knoedler was a believer, and I know she waits for me in heaven. I can't wait to introduce her to Ma Ma Hart when we all get there. Until then, I plan to take Ma Ma Hart's advice and rejoice each day. She should know best of all how to live. After all, she has had over ninety-one years' worth of one-day-at-a-times.

Study Questions

1. What do you like to do to relax? to have fun?
2. Do you try to do something fun each week? every day?
3. When was the last time you laughed out loud? told a funny joke?
4. Think back to when you were younger. What did you enjoy doing? Could you still do some of those activities today?
5. How can you spend time simply having fun with your baby today?

Part 5

Nourishing Mom

Renewing, Restoring, Reviving

Little Girls

What are little girls made of?
Sugar and spice,
And everything nice,
That's what little girls are made of.

Little Boys

What are little boys made of?
Frogs and snails,
And puppy dog tails,
That's what little boys are made of.

Renewing Your Faith

The Spiritual Life of a Mom

Water from the Word

Do everything without complaining or arguing, so that you
may become blameless and pure, children of God without fault
in a crooked and depraved generation, in which you shine like
stars in the universe as you hold out the word of life.

PHILIPPIANS 2:14–16

I was raised in a wonderful, loving home by parents who taught me right from wrong, but I didn't know Christ. Our Christmas and Easter celebrations focused primarily on Santa Claus and the Easter bunny. In junior high, I went through a phase where I attended church with friends and even joined the youth group. It didn't last long; sleeping in on Sunday mornings trumped everything else.

My life was permanently changed in college. In a statistics class at Baldwin-Wallace, a young student named Mike sat about seven rows behind me—hardly in my line of sight. But every time the professor walked to the back of the room to make a point or show a movie, I turned around to find Mike smiling at me. Those dimples did me in right from the start.

Not being the shy type, I approached Mike one day before class and introduced myself. Our fate was sealed several weeks later when I was at a girlfriend's dorm for a Monday Night Football party and Mike walked into the lobby. It seemed he also had a friend who lived in that dorm, and he was over for the game as well. We sat and talked during the whole game, even placing bets on who would win. I lost and had to help him with some of his statistics homework. It was really just a ploy for a first date—and I was a willing participant.

I began falling in love with him on our first date, and I haven't stopped.

Even though Mike was a football player, he wasn't your stereotypical jock. He was tender, caring, and genuine. He carried my books for me, opened doors for me, and treated me like a princess.

Food for Thought

A Duke University study revealed that praying for others works. They treated 150 heart patients medically, but only half of them were prayed for by congregations around the world.

The group that was prayed for had better recovery rates, fewer complications, and a 50 percent reduction in problems and complications.[1]

Nine out of ten Americans believe in God and consider religion important in their lives, according to national polls.[2]

After we had been dating for several weeks, I noticed one day that he was wearing a sweatshirt with a cross on it that said something about Christ and Camp Luther. My first thought was, *Why would someone wear a shirt with a cross on it?* Up until then, his faith in Christ had never come up in conversation, and I had never asked.

The next moment is forever etched in my heart. Mike turned to me, the swivel chair he was sitting in squeaking like a train braking on its tracks. He said, "Trish, there's something I need to know."

My mind immediately set to

wandering. *Does he wonder if I'm free for dinner? Want to know if I color my hair?*

Mike continued, "I've accepted Jesus Christ as my Lord and Savior, and I need to know where your heart is, what you believe, and whether or not you're willing to learn about Christ and come to church with me."

Wow! Talk about laying it on the line. The hair-dye question would have been a lot easier to answer. My heart was beating fast, and I had a lump in my throat.

"Well," I said slowly, "I'm not sure what I believe."

It was true. I wasn't sure about the whole Christ thing at that point. But I did know one thing: I wanted to go out with Mike.

"Would you be willing to come to church with me and learn more about Jesus?" Mike asked.

Talk about being put on the spot. Still, I was open to the possibility. "Sure," I said quietly. "I can do that."

Over the next year, I attended Mike's family church every Sunday and saw firsthand what faith in Christ was all about. During that time, Mike never pushed his faith on me. He simply introduced me to the Christ of his heart and let me make my own decision. One year later, I accepted Christ as my Savior, sitting all alone on the bluff of Lake Erie, watching the sun set.

Even if Mike and I hadn't ended up married, he still would have given me the greatest gift of my life. He led me to the cross—patiently, quietly, lovingly—and I'm forever grateful.

Fitting Faith In with a New Baby

It was easier to fit faith into my life before I became a mother. I could read my daily devotions over a leisurely breakfast, attend Bible studies, and spend time with Christian friends whenever I wanted. Mike and I could also spend time in the evenings talking about how things were going at work, whom we were praying for, and how we could pray for each other.

But as a new mother, I found my life controlled by my baby's schedule. I was sleep-deprived, short on patience, and skipping prayer and devotional time. My reasoning went like this: if I couldn't spend twenty minutes in God's Word, why even bother?

Over the years, however, I discovered that if anyone needs God's grace and guidance, it's a mother. Getting out of bed several times a night to feed a newborn is enough to make you just about lose your mind. If you have a baby and older children, then you have to get breakfast on the table, get them dressed, and possibly off to school. Yikes! How do you do all that without the help of God?

So I don't fit faith in perfectly. What I do instead is fit Jesus in. He can be part of everything I do, everything I say. I can pray to Jesus throughout my day and ask for His help, guidance, and forgiveness. That is doable for a busy mom.

Now, instead of feeling guilty about not being able to attend Bible studies or do my devotions every day, I find simple ways to fit faith into daily life. For example, I always have a devotional in the magazine rack in our bathroom. (That's right, moms. It may be the only private time you get, so take advantage of it!) When my children were babies, instead of reading nursery rhymes to them, I sometimes read my devotional aloud. They loved the fact

Food for Thought
Studies show that spirituality is linked to higher marital satisfaction and lower blood pressure.[3]

that I was reading to them, and I enjoyed the added bonus of squeezing in my devotional time. I pray for my husband and my children individually as I fold their laundry, and I pray with my girlfriends over the telephone in moments of desperation and dirty diapers.

Don't let the fact that you can't fit your spiritual time in "perfectly" right now keep you from fitting it in at all. Find moments each day, grab on to them, and watch God weave His blessings into your life!

Barn Siding and Shining Stars

God wants so much more for us than to just "get by." He wants us to "shine like stars in the universe" (Philippians 2:15) to our husbands, our children, and the world around us.

When some mothers think about that, they feel pressure to perform, as if they have to produce the light themselves. They mistakenly believe they have to glow and sparkle and shine like stars on their own volition. As a result, they *always* feel inadequate and insecure, because on our own, we shine more like penlights than stars.

In the corner of my farmhouse kitchen sits a piece of barn siding, weather worn and full of holes and slits from end to end. I keep it in my kitchen as a constant reminder of *who I am*. Here's what I mean: When you walk into a barn on a warm day, the sunbeams shine brilliantly through

Food for Thought
In a recent survey, 43 percent of Americans said they pray for their own health. Twenty-four percent said they have been prayed for by others.[4]

all the cracks and holes in the barn siding. That sprawling light looks so beautiful as it floats in the air, lighting up the darkened barn.

We are like that barn siding. We have holes in our souls and imperfections from end to end. And it is God who shines His light through us. We are not the source of the light; He is. All we have to do is let Him in so He can shine through us. The amazing thing is that the more imperfections, flaws, and holes in our souls, the more opportunity God has to shine His light through us.

Ultimately, it's not about shining your own light. It's about letting God shine through you as brightly as a star in the universe.

FAITH ON FIRE

Dear Lord,

I know most days I probably look more like a penlight than a star shining in the universe. I know I put You second in my life at times when I need to put You first. Help me stay in constant relationship with You throughout each day as I read Your Word and pray my way through my day. And with every mistake I make, help me remember that You shine Your light right through me. Even though I sometimes feel like a piece of old barn siding, all cracked and full of holes, You are warmer and brighter than the sun, and Your light shines through every crack and crevice in my soul.

In Jesus's name,

amen.

Shelter from the Storm

Motherhood is an enormous responsibility.
You are the one who will introduce your child to Christ and build his foundation for faith. Make God an everyday topic of conversation, even when your children are babies. When they wonder at the clouds, say, "Isn't God amazing for giving us the clouds?"

—LIZ G.

One day when my baby was about nine months old,
she was having a screaming fit just as I was trying to clean up the
kitchen so we could head out the door. I decided to put her in the
playpen safely upstairs where she could cry, but I didn't have to hear her.
She cried, then played while I loaded the dishwasher, wiped down
counters, swept the floor, and even got dressed. After only a half hour,
we left a happy baby, happy mom, clean kitchen.

—HEATHER I.

Reach out to other mothers through a local MOPS group,
a Bible study that provides child care, or some other mom-friendly
organization. There's something encouraging about being
surrounded by women facing the same struggles as you.

—LORI S.

FIRST-AID KIT

How to Shine Like a STAR:

☆ **S: Serve others.** Service begins at home. It begins by serving your husband and children, by being the wife and mother God wants you to be. Motherhood can sometimes feel repetitive and boring. Remember that you are not serving just your family; you are serving Christ. You are a missionary, and your mission field is your home.

☆ **T: Take time for God.** This is a challenge for any mom with a busy life. I've learned to pray my way through my day. When I'm washing my son's jeans, trying desperately to scrub the grass stains out of the knees, I thank the Lord for giving me His strength, energy, and love of life. When I'm mopping my kitchen floor, I thank the Lord for the time we enjoy together as a family in our kitchen, and I pray for His grace and protection on each of my children.

☆ **A: Accept your doubts.** Remember that doubting your faith is not the same as unbelief. Rather, it is searching, seeking, and believing that God will meet you where you are. Additionally, don't try to pull your children along to your faith too quickly; it could turn them off to God. Instead, slowly introduce them to the Christ of your heart in a way they'll comprehend and appreciate.

☆ **R: Raise relationships above agendas.** Try to prioritize your relationships over your agenda. This is a daily struggle for me, since I'm a to-do list kind of gal. But I realized long ago that my kids need a relaxed home more than they desire a perfect home. The chores will always be there, but your kids won't. Just remember: people are more important than stuff, and our days this side of heaven are numbered. How do you want to spend them?

S.O.S.
(SPIRITUAL OPPORTUNITY TO SAVOR)

Shout for joy to the LORD, all the earth.
Worship the LORD with gladness;
come before him with joyful songs.
Know that the LORD is God.
It is he who made us, and we are his;
we are his people, the sheep of his pasture.
Enter his gates with thanksgiving
and his courts with praise;
give thanks to him and praise his name.
For the LORD is good and his love endures forever;
his faithfulness continues through all generations.

PSALM 100

What Are You Running Toward?

Even before I accepted Jesus as my Savior, He knew me. As I look back over my life, I realize that I was searching for Him. The problem was that I didn't quite know what I was searching for. I was always looking ahead of me, running at my own pace, expecting God to keep up with my agenda.

But God was there, present in my life even back then. He was molding me, forming me, making me into who I am. Through every trial, God grew my heart. God used every bump in the road to glorify His kingdom through little old me.

The summer before I started junior high, I began having nightmares about attending school there. In one nightmare, I would show up to school in nothing but my shoes. In another, I was lost and no one would help me. I was so nervous that I stressed over it daily that summer. I hardly slept at all.

But I knew there was a God, and I knew He would listen to me. So one night before I closed my eyes to sleep, I said a prayer. And God heard my prayer. My nightmares finally stopped, and when I did start junior high in the fall, I discovered new friends, new sports teams, and a lot of fun.

Even before I knew Christ, I prayed. Even before I knew God, He knew me. He created me. He loved me. He was there through it all.

Now that I'm a Christian, I sometimes wonder if my life might have been different had I known Jesus during my growing-up years. But I can't spend time looking back. I have to travel the road in front of me now, the path God has laid out just for me.

Study Questions

1. Have you accepted Jesus as your Savior?
2. What does your faith mean to you? to your family?

3. Do you remember a prayer God answered? How did you feel?

4. Have you ever felt far from God, as if He didn't care about you? Did you have someone you could talk to?

5. How can you incorporate your faith into your daily life as a mom?

Restoring Your Health

The Physical Life of a Mom

Water from the Word
Charm is deceptive, and beauty is fleeting;
but a woman who fears the LORD is to be praised.
PROVERBS 31:30

As a high-school student, I played varsity basketball, volleyball, and even softball for a couple of years.

I am still an athlete at heart, but physically, I am not quite what I used to be. The early mommy years are spent either pregnant, nursing, or grabbing as much sleep as you can, which typically translates to weight gain. Women's bodies go up and down in pounds and size, and I was no exception. Of course, we expect them to bounce right back to their original state, right? Well, that didn't happen to me.

The Old Quilt

An old quilt sits folded in an ancient wicker trunk in our family room. It is as old as the wind, as warm as the sun, and as loved as a mom. The edges are all worn and tattered. The multicolored cloth is tearing, and there are numerous holes starting to shred. It is not a beautiful quilt, to say the least. The striped fabric of red, orange, maroon, yellow, green, and black seems to be as mismatched as a clown's baggy pants. But to us, it is beautiful.

Mike's great-aunt Elta made the quilt for him when he was just a boy, and it now graces our family room. I never met Aunt Elta and probably couldn't pick her out of a family photo album. But I picture her easily. She was a warm, loving person, with a little bit of sass and spark in her. All of these traits are reflected in the colorful pattern of the quilt.

Great-aunt Elta has impacted our family in a very personal way. She created something that keeps my family warm and snuggled together with love. Every hand-sewn stitch was done because she took the time and effort to piece the quilt together.

Mike sometimes says, "Aunt Elta is probably rolling over in her grave when she sees how worn and tattered her quilt has become." But I always respond by saying, "Well, she knows that we are using it and that it is loved."

Like the much-loved Velveteen Rabbit, we have loved that quilt until it is real. It's the first thing my kids ask for when they are sick. It works even better than Tylenol to bring down a fever, and it is the best roof we have found for a rainy-day fort. Our old quilt has heard so many bedtime stories it has probably lost count, and when it whispers goodnight to us, I'm sure I hear "goodnight noises everywhere" (the last line in our

Food for Thought

The best way to lose pregnancy weight, according to *Babytalk* magazine, is to:

Be ready to change. Only when you are ready will anything work.

Embrace proven health habits. Eat less, eat healthfully, exercise.

Give yourself a break. If you slip up, don't give up; just begin again.

Have a cheering section. Ask your family and friends to cheer you on.[1]

favorite book *Goodnight Moon*). It's also very sturdy. It has survived spilled milk, juice stains, and graham cracker crumbs.

Sometimes I think that we should replace our old quilt with something prettier. After all, we have other blankets ranging from soft fleece to warm crochets in that old wicker trunk (and most are in better shape than Great-aunt Elta's quilt). But her quilt has a beauty that can't be compared.

 Food for Thought

TOP TEN THINGS TO DO WITH YOUR PREPREGNANCY JEANS:

1. Hem them and make pants for the baby.
2. Lengthen them and make pants for your husband.
3. Burn them in the backyard fire pit, and roast some hot dogs and make s'mores over them.
4. Use them to patch your husband's torn jeans.
5. Cut them up for burp cloths.
6. Hang them on the fridge for weight-loss motivation.
7. Bury them in a time capsule, along with your white silk shirts and size 34A bra.
8. Hang them on the clothesline, so people driving by still think you can fit into them.
9. Save them for your child's teenage years as proof that you were once cool.
10. Lose the weight and wear 'em.[2]

Good Old Mom

In many ways I think I'm getting to be a lot like our old quilt: worn and tattered around the edges, shredded in places, and stretched beyond my capabilities. And on most days I don't think of myself as beautiful. When I look in the mirror, I see a graying, slightly overweight mom with too many stretch marks and worry wrinkles, usually dressed in khakis and a T-shirt.

But that's not how Mike or my kids see me. They think I'm as beautiful as that old quilt, every fabric full of color and vibrancy. They see me as beautiful inside and out—tattered edges, stretch marks, and all.

My kids think I can cure the common cold with a hug and a glass of ginger ale. Snuggling with Mommy on the couch is usually the first thing they ask for when they wake up in the morning. My hugs work even better than Tylenol to bring down a fever.

As a mom, I survive stains of all sorts on a daily basis, from spilled milk to graham crackers. The daily wear and tear on my body makes me feel worn and tattered at times, but those things also make me who I am: a mom.

Food for Thought

Heart disease is the number one cause of death in the United States today.

Each year 25.6 million Americans are diagnosed with heart disease, which is about 12 percent of the population.

Lack of exercise is the number one factor leading to heart disease.[3]

No one promised that life as a mom would be easy or glamorous, and it isn't. No one told me that after having a baby I would be built like Gwyneth Paltrow or Catherine Zeta-Jones, though I wish I were. No one said I would lose all my pregnancy weight or gain my self-esteem back immediately, and I haven't.

It took me nine months to gain forty pounds with each baby, and I was unable to lose it all before each new baby came along. Granted, most of the time I was too exhausted to care.

Even now, ten years and four kids later, I'm still trying to get my body back into shape. Doing so is a lifelong process, and I'm not just talking about the extra weight. It's also about taking care of your physical health, your emotional health, and your overall well-being.

I don't like being overweight, but I love being a mom. I love all of the rips, tears, and patches life brings to the job. I may not be as old as the wind, but I hope I bring the warmth of the sun to my family.

Exercise should be as essential to our lives as eating or drinking. But if we miss lunch one day, we don't get frustrated and say, "That's it! I'm never eating lunch again!" We go ahead and eat supper, and the next day we get back on track with eating lunch. So why is it that once we start an exercise routine, we get frustrated if we miss a session? This often leads to giving up altogether. What we must remember is that we simply can't *afford* to give up; we now have a little one counting on us to set an example and maintain a positive approach to healthful living.

As you work on getting your body back in shape, you also need to work on accepting who you are, right where you are. As you do, you'll find that along with acceptance will come energy and encouragement.

Blob of a Mom

Here is where you all have to come clean. So take off your shoes and step on the scale. Go ahead—I won't peek at the numbers. What? You don't want to? Me either!

Yes, there are days when I feel like a blob of a mom, all jiggly and wobbly. I could blame it on my four pregnancies, but a lot of it is simply because since I started having children, I haven't stuck to a regular exercise routine for longer than a year. My routine is: start one, it goes well, and then something comes up (like getting pregnant again), and I stop.

Now that I'm done having babies, I have no more excuses.

After Hannah was born, I joined a step aerobics class three mornings a week. I got up early, nursed her, and carted her off in her carrier to the local YMCA. By the end of the year, I had lost a lot of baby weight and was down two sizes.

Then the stick turned blue again.

I continued attending class for a while and just toned down my workout, but before I knew it my belly had grown. It just wasn't any fun juggling that big thing around or stepping up and down more often than I had to. So I quit.

After Sydney was born, I did nothing (unless you count walking up and down the stairs carrying twenty pounds of clean laundry exercise). With all of that stair climbing, you'd think my legs would look like Elle Macpherson's; but lo and behold, they don't.

Once again motherhood called when I became pregnant with Colin. During those crazy nine months we also renovated our century-old farmhouse from top to bottom, so I was more wrapped up in choosing lighting fixtures and wall colors than exercising. I gained another forty pounds, my shoe size went up, and my self-confidence went down.

After Colin was born, I started walking with my friend Teri at night after the kids were in bed. We would drive to the high school and walk around the track as we chitchatted about life. The conversation meant even more to me than the exercise, and we usually made it two to three miles before heading home.

Then Riley came, and things got even crazier. Life with four kids hardly gives me time to breathe, let alone exercise. But I bought a Pilates tape and diligently started getting up at the crack of dawn to do my thirty-minute workout. I did it every day, seven days a week. And yes, I toned up and went down a size. Then I quit.

I have tried it all, from walking to running to step aerobics to Pilates. I have also eaten frozen cookie dough at 3 a.m. after feeding

Food for Thought

Though physical activity is vital to losing weight and staying healthy, 59 percent of American adults do not engage in physical activity outside work three or more times a week.[4]

a screaming newborn and needing a sugar spike. I am not the perfect dieter. I am not the perfect exerciser. And I am not the perfect mom.

But I've discovered the key to success: *choose what works for you and then work at it*. If that means popping baby in the backpack and strolling around the block, do it. If you are a runner, take your baby out for a spin in the jogging stroller. If you want to stay home, purchase a couple of exercise DVDs and do them while your baby naps. If you want to work out with friends, join the local YMCA (most offer free child care during specific workout sessions).

I don't believe what you do matters as much as doing something and not giving up. Remember, managing weight and staying in shape are lifelong endeavors. It is a journey, not a destination.

Food for Thought

A 1997 *Psychology Today* survey revealed that more than half (56 percent) of women worldwide are dissatisfied with their overall appearance.

More specifically, 71 percent aren't happy with their abdomens; 60 percent hate their hips. Regarding weight, 60 percent aren't happy with theirs and 89 percent want to lose weight.

The average woman's weight is 140 pounds, and the overall preferred weight they desire is 125 pounds.[5]

Eye of the Beholder

I once heard Christian author and speaker Anita Renfroe joke that she suffers from reverse anorexia: she is thinner in her mind than she is in reality.

I have the same affliction. I'll be walking into the grocery store, suddenly catch a glimpse of my reflection in the window, and think, *Wow, am I fat! Guess I won't be buying any Oreos today!*

But at thirty-nine, I have also accepted who I am and how I'm built. And I'm forever thankful that my husband loves me as is (though I'm convinced he pretends I'm shaped like Julia Roberts, bless his imaginative little heart). I'm not giving up, mind you. I'm just accepting my reality while I work on improving that reality.

My friend Carla once said that one of the reasons she loves me is that I'm so comfortable in my own skin. There is a lot of truth in this. I like who I am, and I am okay as is. I think that is where we all have to start.

How God Sees Us

We have become a weight-conscious society, valuing thinness over even life itself.

Research on body image and weight found that 15 percent of women and 11 percent of men would sacrifice more than five years of their lives to be the weight they want to be.[6] How terribly sad is that? People are willing to give away years this side of heaven so they can be…thin? I think these people have severely messed-up priorities and have lost sight of the gift God gave them in simply being alive.

How do you think God sees you? Do you think He cares what size your thighs are? What size your belly is, or whether you fit into size 6 jeans?

God has x-ray vision: He sees through your skin right to your heart. He wants you to love and fear Him. He desires that you find your beauty in His beauty and in His love. *That's* my biggest hope and prayer for each of you.

Of course, He wants us to be healthy, and losing weight and exercising are great places to begin. But keep in mind that God is more concerned with your inner beauty. Even the prettiest people you know will someday get wrinkled and gray, and begin to sag and bag in places they never knew existed.

Go ahead and join a gym. Start with a walk around the block, do step aerobics, or jog for miles. Because I want you to live a long and lovely life, I want you to be healthy. But never forget who you are, and never forget that you are beautiful no matter what size jeans you are wearing.

FAITH ON FIRE

Dear Lord,

Thank You for my beautiful body, for creating me in Your image, and for loving me just as I am. Help me discover the beauty within my heart as I love my husband, my children, and You. Help me rediscover the beauty I have on the outside as I challenge myself to lose my pregnancy weight and get back into shape. Go with me to the gym, hang out with me at the YMCA, accompany me for a walk around the block, and help me feel Your loving arms each step of the way.

In Jesus's name,

amen.

Shelter from the Storm

Oh puhleeze, my body has never been the same. Rather than look at it as having flaws, I see it as having history.

—BRENDA N.

Yes, there are stretch marks—tons! I gained forty pounds with each pregnancy, and I haven't lost it all yet! I left the hospital wearing maternity clothes....but I have learned to accept myself for who I am and simply do the best I can to lose weight.

—LYNETTE M.

I was surprised at how much weight I gained with each pregnancy.
I'd never had a problem with my weight, but during pregnancy
I was starving—I mean, I couldn't sleep unless I got up and
made a turkey sandwich. I usually put on at least thirty to
forty pounds with each pregnancy. It eventually came off,
with lots of exercise. But it was still surprising to me.

—HEATHER I.

Embrace your postnatal curves while trying to lose
that pregnancy weight. It's the best of both worlds!
And remember that you are "fearfully and wonderfully made"
(Psalm 139:14) and that God does not make junk!

—ERIN S.

FIRST-AID KIT

★ **Rock around the clock.** Find a walking buddy and begin walking
together around your block or the local high-school track in the
evenings.

★ **Baby steps.** Exercise with your baby—there are plenty of instruc-
tional DVDs available to show you how. Or simply do sit-ups or
leg lifts while you play with your baby on the floor.

★ **YMCA.** Join your local YMCA and begin attending aerobics or
water aerobics classes. Sometimes it's easier to stick with an exercise routine if you are financially invested in it.

★ **Do the DVD.** There are a ton of exercise DVDs on the market.
Find one that is right for you and exercise in the comfort of
your home.

★ **Buddy.** Ask a girlfriend to hold you accountable and then team up
to meet and exercise regularly. Encourage each other in love.

★ **Do what works for *you*.** Whatever you do, do something physical. Walk, run, do sit-ups, use weights, play racquetball. It really doesn't matter what you do as long as you exercise regularly, increase your heart rate, and get your muscles moving.

S.O.S.
(SPIRITUAL OPPORTUNITY TO SAVOR)

The LORD your God is with you,
he is mighty to save.
He will take great delight in you,
he will quiet you with his love,
he will rejoice over you with singing.

ZEPHANIAH 3:17

 Mirror, Mirror, on the Wall

Okay, here goes the honest part of me speaking. *I am overweight.* There, I said it. Worse, it's in print for all to see.

I don't like my plump belly that I can never get flat again. I don't like that my thighs jiggle when I walk or run. I don't like the flab that hangs down from my arms, and I don't like being the size that I am. I don't want to preach to you about losing weight, because I am still a work in progress myself. But I'm working at it.

A couple of years ago I started going to Curves, a chain of exercise clubs only for women. They weigh you, measure everything, and do monthly updates, and they recommend a minimum of three workouts a week. I lost some weight that year, but because they don't offer baby-sitting and I still had Riley at home, I had to work out at 6 a.m. before Mike left for work. I ran myself ragged trying to keep that schedule.

The next summer I rode my bike. I rode up and down hills, here and there. I even rode so far one day that I couldn't make it back, and Mike had to come get me in the minivan (thank the Lord I had my cell phone with me!).

This past year I once again joined a step aerobics class at our YMCA three times a week. I started because my best friend, Carla, was teaching the class, and before I knew it, I was addicted. I have lost some weight and some inches, which is encouraging. But I still have a long way to go, and that's okay too. I'm headed in the right direction, I have greater energy and a better attitude, and I've improved my health.

Keep in mind, I am well into my mothering years and am through having babies. I am now in the recovery phase of motherhood, trying to get my body back to some sense of normalcy. But during those early mommy years when you are pregnant and nursing, and pregnant again and nursing again, it can be difficult to fit exercise in.

So here's my best advice: *just do it*. Walk, run, bike, swim, hike, do step aerobics. Whatever you can squeeze in, do it. And if it isn't every day, that's fine. Do what you can.

No matter what kind of shape you are in, God delights in you. It's a done deal, as is, no changes or exchanges needed. God takes delight in you, inside and out. You were created in His image.

Remember, He loves you as you are—but He also wants what is best for you. I know that I'll never be a size 4. What I *can* be is the best me possible. I can get into better shape and improve my physical health. That is what I'm working on.

Study Questions

1. When was the last time you went for a walk? a run?
2. Do you remember when you used to be in better shape?

3. Do you have a girlfriend you could ask to exercise with you? someone who can encourage you?

4. Write down three things you can do to get moving again. Now get going!

Reviving Your Friendships

The Emotional Life of a Mom

Water from the Word
Two are better than one,
because they have a good return for their work:
If one falls down,
his friend can help him up.
ECCLESIASTES 4:9–10

She was my best friend. You know the one. The girlfriend who wrote "friends forever" at the bottom of every note you passed in sixth-grade study hall. The one who sat four seats up and two seats over in those fake wood desks between the moldy-smelling books in the junior high library.

Her name is Lisa. We met in sixth-grade English class, and from that moment on we were joined at the hip. We spent many sleepless nights at each other's houses, talking, giggling, and growing up. We dreamed about this boy or that, and could hardly wait until we were both old enough to date. We both fell in love in high school with the "man of our dreams" and thought it was for keeps—only to discover that love is complicated and maybe we needed time to figure it all out.

We graduated from college with huge smiles, big plans, and an entire lifetime ahead of us.

After that, we grew apart. Our Christmas card exchange faltered, and before I knew it, nine years had flown by.

Then she "passed me a note"—this time by e-mail rather than a handwritten letter in study hall. We spent a few months chatting online and catching up on the changes we'd each experienced over the years. Finally, I decided to pack up my two preschoolers and hit the highway, so we could meet for lunch and get reacquainted in person.

When she opened the front door, her smile warmed my heart. Our boys hit it off amazingly well as they tackled the playroom, going from one toy to another.

She hadn't prepared a fancy lunch—just pasta with sliced apples on the side. But it tasted like a meal at the Ritz to me. We sat and talked for hours in between filling juice cups, checking on the boys, and changing diapers.

I guess it surprised me how instantly comfortable we were with each other—kind of like slipping your foot into a soft, cozy slipper. That day I realized that many things in life do remain the same, even through life's chaotic changes.

When it was time to leave, we hugged and promised to get together that spring. Then the most amazing thing happened: Lisa told me that I looked just like I did in high school. I was thinking the same thing about her! Since we have both undeniably aged, I realize that we were looking at each other's hearts, not the wrinkles at the corners of our eyes. Hearing it from her felt great anyway.

I stepped back in time that day. It was nice to be young again. Although Lisa and I probably won't have any more giggling sleepovers, we are blessed that the "men of our dreams" are now our husbands and that this time love is for keeps.

We still have huge smiles and big plans. We also have busy days filled with children and laughter. We may no longer be joined at the hip, but we can still be joined at the heart, even across the miles. Whenever I need to feel young again, all I have to do is pass her a note through e-mail and open the door to forever friendship.

Food for Thought
On average, men spend 10 hours a week with their friends, while women spend just 7.5 hours a week with theirs.[1]

Friends Forsaken

Girlfriends are very important in our lives—more than we probably realize. When we don't take the time to stay close to our girlfriends, we lose out on treasures.

If you ask any eight-year-old girl who her best friend is, a name will be on the tip of her tongue. This is because little girls *understand* the importance of friendship. They eat lunch together in the cafeteria, share secrets on the playground, and have tons of giggling sleepovers.

But something happens when we grow up. We let go of those little-girl ways and let our friendships slip away.

Research shows that men spend ten hours a week with their friends while women spend just seven and a half. But men don't "talk" to their friends. So what are they doing?

Men may have more friend time because some of that time is spent at work or at play. Studies reveal that "men's friendships are based on doing things, such as playing a team sport. Women's friendships are based on talking and sharing feelings."[2]

When we are young, we make time for friends. When we go off to college, we spend time with friends. When we get married, we still try to squeeze our girlfriends into our lives…but it gets tougher and tougher.

Then we become moms, and when that first baby arrives, the first priority to slip is usually our girlfriends. A landmark UCLA study concludes, "Every time we get overly busy with work and family, the first thing we do is let go of friendships with other women…we push them right to the back burner."[3] When we need them most, we let them go. When we need someone to help and support us, we isolate ourselves in our homes with our babies.

The same study describes how men and women react differently to stress. When men face stress, they lean toward "fight or flight"; but women, researchers discovered, "tend and befriend." Why?

A common response to stress for women is the release of a hormone called oxytocin, which produces a calming effect. This allows women to tend to their children and befriend others in the stressful situation.

Nothing is more stressful than bringing home your first baby from the hospital and realizing you are in charge of this helpless human being, this tiny bundle of love! Combine that with little sleep at night, breasts filled with milk, racing hormones, and postpregnancy blues, and *wham!* you need a friend.[5]

Food for Thought

Research has shown that the more friends a woman has, the less likely she is to develop physical impairments as she ages and the more likely she is to lead a joyful life.

In fact, statistics conclude that not having close girlfriends is as bad for your health as smoking or being overweight.[4]

So how do you do it? How do you juggle all the demands of motherhood and keep your friends close as well? To begin with, make at least one short phone call to a friend every day. Schedule a quiet night out with your girlfriends once a month. And finally, don't underestimate the power of e-mail.

Friends Found

The first place I found girlfriends after becoming a mom was at Mothers of Preschoolers (MOPS).[6] I had heard about MOPS on a local Christian radio station and decided to check it out. Hannah was only two months old, and already I was feeling isolated and trapped at home.

Mike and I had recently moved back to his hometown and onto his family farm; my in-laws lived just up the hill from us. Mike knew everyone in town—he had either grown up with them, knew their family, or had family ties with them. There I was, in the middle of this amazingly beautiful farmland with hills and valleys and plenty of down-home hospitality. And yet I felt alone.

So I went to the MOPS Web site and searched for a group meeting nearby. I still remember walking in with Hannah, because I didn't want to take her to the nursery with all those other babies (you know, the ones with runny noses and all kinds of germs! Ah, I was such a first-time mom). Immediately, another mother came over to greet me. Then a second mom asked if she could hold Hannah while I fixed a plate of something to eat.

They welcomed me as if we were long-lost friends.

That was over twelve years ago, and I'm still a MOPS mom. I have met women there whom I hope to share friendship with for a lifetime. Some are stay-at-home moms; some work outside the home. We come from many different faith backgrounds and lifestyles. But when we meet together, you'd never know how different we are.

Variety is the Spice of Life

Over the last thirty-nine years, I have had many friends come and go in my life. I have also learned that not every friend is the same and not every friendship can be maintained at the same level. And that's okay.

When I was younger, I wanted everyone to like me, to be my best friend. Big surprise—not everyone likes me. (Don't ask me why.)

These early mommy years when you have a baby can be some of the loneliest years you will have. Once your kids get older and start school, you will discover that their friends have—yes, you guessed it—*moms* that you can also befriend. Most of my social life revolves around my kids' activities, and so most of my friendships are with the moms at those activities. It's convenient, and it works.

I just spent tonight sitting with Audrey and Nancy at Sydney's ball game, and in between innings and at bats, we had over two hours of girlfriend time to talk and relate. The only thing missing was a mocha latte…well, maybe next game.

So what kinds of friendships are out there for moms? They might be closer than you think.

Husbands. I think sometimes we women forget that we have a built-in best friend living right under the same roof—our husband. Take the time to talk to your husband, share your feelings and even your funny stories with him. Don't neglect the friendship side of your marriage.

Childhood friends. A lifelong friend is someone you met as a child who you still stay in touch with. These kinds of friendships are not easy to come by, so if you have a close girlfriend whom you've known since braces, keep her around. Even if you live miles apart, don't give up on that friendship. After all, she knew you when you had pimples and loved you anyway, so I'd say she's a keeper!

Neighbors. There is something to be said for proximity. When you live next door to or near someone, you will see that person a lot. If you click at all, you will soon become friends. Teri was my neighbor long before we became best friends, but it didn't take long to discover that we had a lot in common. We make each other laugh, we help each other out, and on a good day, I stop over for a hot cup of coffee and a smile.

Don't underestimate the power of your neighbor friends. Look around your neighborhood and find a mom whom you can befriend. Who knows? You might be just what she is looking for and what you both need.

Family. When you are young, your mom and dad are your whole world. But soon enough, that world grows. You discover friends at school and at church, and you kind of forget about family. (This often happens during the teen years, when Mom and Dad are very uncool and friends rule.)

But, as you grow up, you discover that Mom and Dad are kind of cool again. You can actually forge friendships with your parents and yes, even your in-laws. Before you know it, you'll have some pretty great friends!

Food for Thought

FIVE IDEAS FOR FINDING FRIENDS

1. Go online and find the nearest moms' group meeting near you and jump in. You will never find a better place to be at home than with other moms.

2. You may have a neighbor who feels as isolated as you, trapped at home with a baby or toddler. Invite her over for coffee.

3. If you work outside of your home, look around for other moms like you. Together you can make time for friendship.

4. Next Sunday morning, scan the sanctuary for all the moms with babies in their arms or toddlers on their hips. Get to know a few and ask them to get together once a month or so. Don't forget to see what kinds of organized groups your church offers that could mean friendship and support for young moms.

5. Rekindle those friendships you keep kicking yourself for letting go of. Even if they live far away, you can stay in touch by e-mail or phone.

Girlfriends. Girlfriends are the women we adore, the ones we gripe to when things go wrong, the friends we call the minute the baby begins to walk on his own. They cry with us, laugh with us, pray for us, and see us through most of life's ups and downs. We don't nearly appreciate them enough, and usually we need them more than we realize. Don't ever underestimate the power of this kind of friendship—the kind in which your girlfriend can see your house in a mess and you in your pj's with messy hair and no makeup.

FAITH ON FIRE

Dear Lord,
Thank You for the gift of friendship and the gift of sisters, who are related by both blood and heart. As we struggle to find the time for friendships in our lives, remind us to be a friend first. As we love, encourage, and support our friends, help us remember that You are nourishing us as well.
In Jesus's name,
amen.

Shelter from the Storm

The worst part of having a newborn is that I sometimes
feel very disconnected from others (I stay at home)
and trapped in my own house.
—*ALLISON L.*

Before the baby, I had very high expectations for what
I could accomplish in one day. Now I'm impressed if I accomplish
in one week what I could do in one day before.
—*LEAH R.*

*Give yourself permission to feel frustrated when your child cries
and you are stressed or drained by it. Just know that you can
feel frustrated without having to act on those feelings.*

—ALLISON L.

*When you need a hand, other moms are generally ready
and willing to step up and help you out. Just be sure you
return the favor—it's a give-and-take type of relationship.*

—LORI S.

*My entire social life now revolves around my kids' school field trips
and their evening baseball games. Most of my girlfriends are the
parents of my kids' friends. It makes sense. That's who I am
around most of the time, and we have so much in common.*

—KATIE C.

FIRST-AID KIT

Seven Ways to Find Happiness

1. **Take control of your time.** When you have a baby, for the
   first time since childhood you are not in control of your
   life. But you can control some things. You can ask for help
   and take little breaks from motherhood, like going to the
   library for one hour just to read a book in quiet, or letting
   your husband bathe the baby so you can take a walk
   around the block.

2. **Act happy.** Sometimes the first step in actually being happy
   is to act happy. According to therapist David G. Myers,
   "Although self-esteem, optimism, and extroversion tend to
   be enduring traits, those who seek greater happiness can

exploit one of social psychology's arch principles: We are as likely to act ourselves into a way of thinking as to think ourselves into action." In other words—*fake it!*

3. **Seek to engage your skills.** When you first bring home that bundle of joy, you can hardly think beyond the next feeding or diapering, let alone recall things you used to enjoy doing. God has given you so many gifts, talents, and loves, and He wants you to use them however He calls you to do so. It might be as simple as taking one evening a week to work on your scrapbooking or to paint a picture if you love art. Perhaps reading a good book or taking photographs will make you feel better.

4. **Join the movement movement.** The last thing you want to think about as you drag your saggy, baggy, just-delivered-a-baby body home from the hospital is exercise, right? I'm right there with you. But exercise is important to your overall health and well-being. Start very small, with little walks up and down your driveway. As your body heals from delivering your baby, begin walking around the block or stretching out your arms and legs while the baby rests on a blanket nearby.

5. **Get rest.** No, this is not a joke. Even God rested on the seventh day, which emphasizes how important rest was. Ask for help, and take help when it is offered. A great place to start is with grandparents and girlfriends: let them pinch hit so you can sneak a nap in here and there.

6. **Prioritize relationships.** At this moment in time, no one is closer to you than your baby. But it's important that you don't isolate yourself during these critical first months of motherhood. You need to spend time with other adults,

especially adults you are close to and can confide in. Begin with your husband: try to talk to him every day, even if it is just over the phone. And don't leave out your extended family or your girlfriends.

7. **Take control of the soul.** I believe that God created us to be joy filled. As C. S. Lewis once said, "Joy is the serious business of heaven." It can be difficult to find the time to pray or read the Bible when you have a newborn. But don't neglect your soul, your faith, or God. He wants to be close to you, and He is there to help you through these challenging first months. Find simple ways to include Him, like praying through the day or keeping a Bible within reach.[7]

S.O.S.
(SPIRITUAL OPPORTUNITY TO SAVOR)

Two are better than one,
   because they have a good return for their work:
If one falls down,
   his friend can help him up.
But pity the man who falls
   and has no one to help him up!
Also, if two lie down together, they will keep warm.
   But how can one keep warm alone?
Though one may be overpowered,
   two can defend themselves.
A cord of three strands is not quickly broken.

ECCLESIASTES 4:9–12

Swapping More Than Suppers

Five years ago my friend Carla asked if I wanted to start a supper-swapping group with her. Since my family was tired of grilled cheese, and I knew eating a nutritious meal together as a family was important to our kids, I said yes.

In a nutshell, supper swapping is cooking one day a week in bulk (like making four batches of spaghetti), keeping one meal for your family, and delivering the rest to the friends in your group. The rest of the week, they deliver suppers to you. Yum!

I soon discovered that I loved supper swapping. It greatly simplified mealtimes at our house. I even wrote a book about it so other moms could be blessed like I was. But what surprised me the most was that it blessed my life with deeper friendships as well.

When you put a jigsaw puzzle together, where do you begin? At the edges and corners, right? You snap those pieces in first, and then the bigger picture begins to unfold. Well, supper swapping snapped all the friendship edges and corners into my life. Suddenly I was staying in better touch with my girlfriends, calling them more often, and making time for them in my life.

In Ecclesiastes, God tells us that "two are better than one, because they have a good return for their work: If one falls down, his friend can help him up." But most of us women like to be the one helping someone else up. We like to be the givers. It makes us feel needed, loved, and accepted.

Being the receiver—allowing a friend to help us out—can sometimes make us uncomfortable. It leaves us feeling inadequate and needy, like we now owe them something in return.

But if no one is willing to be the receiver, then there is no one to give to.

So in receiving, you are actually giving: You are giving your girlfriend the chance to help you. And as you join together giving and receiving, you both become stronger—better than one.

Study Questions

1. When was the last time you let one of your girlfriends help you out by baby-sitting your baby? How did that make you feel?

2. When was the last time you helped out a friend? How did that make you feel?

3. Have you thought about simplifying your life a bit by swapping suppers or swapping baby-sitting with a girlfriend?

4. Who are your closest girlfriends? How often do you talk with them?

5. Why do you think God wants us to have friends? How does having friends honor God? bless us?

6. Write down three ways you can make more time for your friendships, and three new places you can look for new friends.

Afterword

Enjoy the Journey

Having a baby is a spellbinding experience: you will find yourself in a daze for much of the first year.

But you aren't just a mom for a year. You are a mom for a *lifetime*. And it's worth every penny. Lots of pennies, in fact. The federal government has rather daze-inducing figures of its own on what it costs to raise a child today. From birth to eighteen, the cost is estimated at around $160,140. This figure doesn't include college tuition, nor does it account for the increasing number of young adults moving home after college.

But when you break it down, $160,140 isn't so bad. It translates into $8,896.67 a year, $741.39 a month, or $171.09 a week. That's a mere $24.44 a day! Just over a dollar an hour.[1]

So here you are, walking on the wild side of life, trying to figure out if you have what it takes to be the mother your child needs, the mom God intended you to be. What do you get for all the diaper changing, sleep deprivation, headaches, and worries?

Well, you get naming rights, for starters—first, middle, and last. You get glimpses of God every morning, and giggles under the covers every night. You get more love than your heart can hold, sticky peanut butter kisses, and arms that fit perfectly around your neck. You get a hand to hold, and someone to remind you that clouds look like dinosaurs and that dandelions make beautiful bouquets. You get to blow bubbles, fly kites, build sandcastles, and jump in mud puddles without caring about the mess.

Every fall you get to rake all the leaves into a great big pile and jump in, carve pumpkins into jack-o'-lanterns, and bake the seeds for a treat. Every summer you get to run barefoot in the grass through the sprinkler, catch lightning bugs, and wonder at the rock collection in your child's bedroom.

And every December you get to play Santa Claus, packing the presents under the tree until no more can fit. You even get the added bonus of eating the cookies and milk left out for the big elf in red. You are reminded that hills were meant for sledding and snow was meant to be piled into a snowman or eaten fresh off the ground.

You get to hang rainbows, hearts, and flowers under refrigerator magnets and collect spray-painted noodle wreaths for Christmas, handprints set in clay for Mother's Day, and I LOVE YOU notes with the letters printed backward. You get to lick the melting ice cream cone in circles so it doesn't drip on that new T-shirt, and you get to watch your children bow their heads and say their bedtime prayers every night.

You get a front-row seat to history—first step, first word, first bra, first date, and first time behind the wheel. You get another branch added to your family tree, and if you're lucky, a long list of limbs called grandchildren. You get an education in psychology, nursing, criminal justice, communications, and human sexuality that no college can match. In the eyes of a child, you rank right up there with God. You have all the power to heal a boo-boo, scare away the monsters under the bed, patch a broken heart, police a slumber party, ground them forever, and love them without limits.

All so one day they, like you, will love without counting the cost.

Best of all, for a mere $160,140 you get to impact the life and soul of a child and introduce her to the Lord and Savior Jesus Christ. And you get to promise to meet her in heaven someday, many years from now.[2]

All in all, a pretty sound investment.

Additional Resources

Twinkle, Twinkle Little Star

Twinkle, twinkle, little star,
How I wonder what you are.
Up above the world so high,
Like a diamond in the sky.
Twinkle, twinkle, little star,
How I wonder what you are.

Discovering the Footprints of Heaven

Hope in the Nursery

Water from the Word
He will cover you with his feathers,
and under his wings you will find refuge;
his faithfulness will be your shield and rampart.

PSALM 91:4

There was no funeral when my baby died. I wasn't able to hold my precious little one or look into his eyes. I didn't get to count his tiny little fingers and toes or kiss his chubby cheeks. My arms ached, because I never had the chance to embrace him and tell him I loved him.

My baby would have been born on February 27, 2002, but he died when I was thirteen weeks along in my pregnancy. I'm not even sure if my baby was a boy or a girl. I was already a mother of three when I had my first miscarriage.

During my time of grief, many well-intentioned family and friends implied that I should get over my loss and on with life. They suggested that I was dwelling on something I had no control over. Some of them reminded me that I should be thankful for the children I already had. After all, I could always have another baby, right?

Though all these things were true, they didn't heal my pain.

Ultrasounds and Ultra Pain

I received the news of my miscarriage at my obstetrician's office. I had gone in for a second-trimester checkup and was feeling great. There was no bleeding or cramping; in fact, I had no signs of trouble at all. But because I was in my midthirties, my obstetrician, Dr. Tizzano, wanted to perform a simple ultrasound to check on the baby, mainly to see if we were having twins.

Then suddenly he turned the screen away from me. My heart sank to my ankles, and I asked what was wrong.

Dr. Tizzano asked me again what my due date was. I told him. Then he asked if I might have miscalculated my period—by an entire month. My baby was not showing a heartbeat yet, and at thirteen weeks there should be one.

My first thought was *Sure, yeah, I probably did miscalculate.* But even as I frantically tried to convince myself the baby was fine, I knew it wasn't the case. My eyes welled up.

Dr. Tizzano put his arm around my shoulder and handed me a tissue. He told me we didn't know anything yet for sure, that he would run some additional blood work and another ultrasound. We should monitor the baby closely for a week or so and see if it had developed further.

He held my hand and began talking numbers, percentages, and probabilities, but all I heard was *blah, blah, blah.* My tears fell faster. My head was spinning, and my heart was breaking.

Is my baby dead? When did this happen? How did it happen? And why?

It felt like a dream, like watching it happen to someone else. I began to pray, asking God to save my baby, give my baby a heartbeat, make this pain go away.

But I received no answer, just silence. I felt so alone.

Finding My Way Home

I walked out of Dr. Tizzano's office and down the hallway, through the maze of twists and turns that led to the outside world. If I could have sprinted without drawing too much attention, I would have. I wanted to get out of there and get home so badly.

Life as I knew it suddenly seemed cold and dangerous.

I located my car in the parking lot, climbed in, and sat in silence for a moment. My mind was racing. My head hurt. My heart felt broken. I locked the door and began to sob—for being all alone, for not knowing what was going to happen, for the baby I might never see this side of heaven.

I must have sat there for twenty minutes, crying, dying on the inside. Finally, I picked up my cell phone and called home. I knew I wouldn't be able to wait until I got home to share my pain with Mike. I had to get it out now.

Mike answered the phone so cheerfully. I could hear the kids playing in the background. It all seemed very surreal.

As soon as I heard Mike's

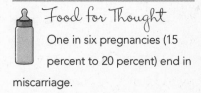

Food for Thought

One in six pregnancies (15 percent to 20 percent) end in miscarriage.

One miscarriage does *not* increase the chance of a second miscarriage.

About 80 percent (four out of five) of spontaneous abortions occur in the first trimester of pregnancy (in the initial 13 weeks of gestation).

By far the most common cause for a miscarriage is a fetal abnormality, and there is nothing anyone can do to prevent it.[1]

voice, I began to sob again. I hated to let him hear me cry, but I couldn't control it. I told him everything that had happened, and he asked if I wanted him to come pick me up. I said no, that I needed some time alone; the half-hour drive home would give me a chance to collect myself. I didn't want to cry in front of the kids and scare them.

Mike was the second man that day who tried to reassure me…and it still didn't work. He reminded me that things might still be okay, that we should wait for the test results before we got too worked up. After we prayed together, I got off the phone, took some deep breaths, and began the drive home.

I thought about my dear friend Audrey, who had miscarried two weeks earlier. At the time I had cried with her, listened to her pain, and reassured her. But in the back of my mind, while Audrey was hurting, all I could think was *Thank You, God, that it's not me. I could never handle a miscarriage!* I couldn't believe how strong and faithful Audrey was. I knew I could never survive that kind of loss.

Yet here I was, in a strange twist of fate, going through the same nightmare. It seemed so unfair. How could God allow this to happen to me and my baby?

Becoming a Vessel God Can Use

What followed were two weeks of tests and ultrasounds, good news and bad news, confusion and sadness. Mike and I prayed for the baby, we prayed for peace and understanding, and we cried a lot.

I searched the Bible for answers, for reflections of understanding, to feel God's love. I claimed Psalm 91:4 as my verse of hope and comfort: "He will cover you with his feathers, and under his wings you will find refuge; his faithfulness will be your shield and rampart."

I needed to find that refuge under His wing. I needed to be covered by His faithfulness since my faith seemed so weak at the moment. I still prayed for a miracle. I wanted my baby to be alive. So that's what I prayed for. I didn't want God's will. I wanted mine. I wanted my baby!

A week later, the doctors were certain that the baby was gone. There had been no growth in over a week. No heartbeat. No movement. But Mike and I wanted confirmation before we scheduled a D and C. That's what we prayed for most: a clear and final answer from God.

Then, in the midst of our anguish and sadness, God gave us our answer. The final ultrasound showed a blank screen.

Our baby was gone. Finally, we had confirmation of miscarriage. The loss was real. Our baby was dead. Our answer was clear.

Food for Thought

According to the American College of Surgeons, "A D and C—also known as dilatation (dil-ah-tay'-shun) and curettage (koo-re-tahzh')—is a minor surgical procedure in which the surgeon first dilates or opens the woman's cervix and then inserts a thin, spoon-shaped instrument…to remove a sample of the internal lining of the uterus or to remove the portion of the internal lining that is causing bleeding."

Many times, a D and C is needed after a miscarriage for the health and safety of the mom. If you think you have had a miscarriage, consult with your obstetrician immediately.[2]

Afterward, neither Mike nor I wanted to go home, so we went to a nearby diner. As I sat in the vinyl booth, quietly grieving, God spoke to me as clearly as if He were sitting next to me. I didn't see a burning bush like Moses did, but God's voice was very real nonetheless. He told me, "My child, don't you realize that I used you as a vessel to bring this little soul to heaven?"

And I felt peace. Right there in that cold vinyl booth at The Green

Leaf diner, I found peace about my miscarriage. I shared the experience with Mike, and warmth filled our booth.

Our sadness wasn't gone completely, nor had we shed our last tears. In fact, I still feel anguish over the loss of the baby. As I wrote these words down over five years later, I cried again for the child I will never get to hold in my arms. But I have an even greater sense of peace and pride. I'm proud that God chose *me* to bring a soul to heaven, and I'm confident that He will hold my precious baby until I can be there myself.

Hope in the Nursery

I have always been a glass-is-half-full kind of gal. I like looking at the positives in my life. I like being joyful.

But after my miscarriage, it was difficult to find my way back to who I was. I had been let down like never before, and lost more than I thought I could lose. Life seemed crueler to me, and I spent many months trying to find my way back to my joyful self.

When we began trying to conceive again, I was very nervous. I wasn't sure I could survive another miscarriage if I had one. I wasn't sure I could face that loss again. But we so wanted another baby, so I prayed and prayed, and we began to try to conceive.

One of the toughest things for me about suffering the miscarriage was that it was completely out of my control. I couldn't fix it. I couldn't save my baby. That same loss of control hit me again when we tried to get pregnant.

One month. Two months. Three months went by, and still no baby. I felt like I would never be pregnant again. After a few more months, Dr. Tizzano suggested we run some tests. We did, and lo and behold, I was not ovulating. It was as if my body had shut down after the miscarriage.

I have known Dr. Tizzano for a long time. He has been my OB for over a decade, back to when we had our first baby. I adore him, and I would trust him with my life. So when he suggested we try a low dose of Clomid to stimulate my body back into ovulation, I didn't hesitate to say yes.

During that first month I was on Clomid, Dr. Tizzano ran some tests to see if I ovulated. Well, I had. In fact, my ovaries released three eggs. Yep, three. Within the week, the pregnancy test came back positive, and Mike and I started to wonder how many babies were in there anyway.

As we pondered the possibility of having triplets, I couldn't help but be elated. However many babies God decided to bless us with, I was just plain excited to be pregnant. Mike did mention that if we had triplets, going from three kids to six, we would have to get bunk beds for the bedrooms and color code everything. It would be like living at summer camp all year round.

Soon enough, we discovered that we were expecting twins. But before that reality had time to sink in, we found out that one of the babies had stopped growing and died early on in the pregnancy. Here we were suffering another miscarriage, saying good-bye to another baby we wouldn't get to hold. This time, however, we were so thankful for the baby who was alive that our sorrow seemed outweighed by our joy.

Food for Thought

"Mommy, please don't cry…
    A beautiful angel carried me here!
I met Jesus today, Mommy.
He cradled me in His big, strong arms.
He made me feel so happy inside…
Someday, Mommy, we will hold each other tight!
Then you will cradle me in your arms,
And stroke my hair…
And once again, our hearts will beat together.
Mommy, please don't cry…
I'll wait right here for you."[3]

On January 8, 2003, our precious little Riley Ann was born. Her baby brother or sister had joined our other baby in heaven.

The Grieving Process

There was no funeral for either of the babies I miscarried. I didn't get to hold their precious bodies or look into their eyes. But God did. He was there. Though my arms will always ache for them, I know that someday I'll get to hold and love them.

If you have suffered the loss of miscarriage, I grieve with you. I wish I were sitting next to you on the couch, so I could put my arms around you and tell you that healing will come and joy will return. I wish I could take away your pain, hold your chin in my hand, look into your eyes, and let you see my own healing.

 Food for Thought
RECOMMENDATIONS FOR HELPING YOU FIND PEACE
AFTER A MISCARRIAGE

Music: Listen to "Glory Baby" by Watermark on the CD *All Things New*.
Book: Read *Mommy, Please Don't Cry* by Linda DeYmaz.
Support: Find a girlfriend who has also experienced a miscarriage and lean on her.
Reach out: When time has healed your heart, find a new mom who is having a miscarriage and let her lean on you.

I would tell you that the pain you are feeling is real. You were not just "a little pregnant"; your loss is real, and healing will take time. I would tell you how proud I am of you for getting out of bed and facing another day without your precious baby. Then I would cry with you, pray with you, and hope with you. And I would let you grieve in your own way and your own time.

Many women will face the loss of miscarriage at some point in their lives. There is nothing I can say in black and white here that will make it easy. But I can assure you that every baby God creates, He creates with a purpose. And occasionally that purpose is for your precious baby to join Him in heaven before he is born.

Sometimes God uses the footprints of our little ones to show us His eternal love. We have to see the hope that lies in the nursery, the everlasting hope of eternal life. Sometimes all we have is the refuge of God's wings—but it's all we need.

And though I still grieve for my glory babies, I know they rest in the arms of the Lord. There is hope in the nursery, even when God's plans aren't our plans. Our hope doesn't come from everything going our way. Our hope comes from knowing the One whose way is best.

FAITH ON FIRE

Dear Lord,
Sometimes I don't understand why bad things happen, why some moms miscarry their babies and others don't. My heart aches for all the lost babies, yet I know they aren't truly lost— they have been found by You.

Whenever I feel pain, sadness, and loss, You cover me with Your feathers, You protect me under Your wings. Help me seek refuge in You. Help me remember that as out of control as the world sometimes feels, You hold Your wings over me and protect me, and someday our tears will be wiped away.
In Jesus's name,
amen.

Shelter from the Storm

I miscarried our fourth pregnancy at twelve weeks.
When my miscarriage began, I called my midwife. I was lying
on the floor and I told her, "I think I'm going to die!" She said,
"You're not going to die. You're going to get your husband to take
you to the hospital, and I'll meet you there." I had to have
a surgical D and C to stop the bleeding. It was a very
difficult time for me, both physically and emotionally.

—HEATHER I.

It really helped me to talk to other moms who had survived
their own miscarriages. They knew exactly how I felt.
It was very comforting.

—JOAN B.

When I had my second miscarriage, I went in for a D and C.
I remember feeling panicked and asking the nurse to check for
the heartbeat one more time to make sure the baby was truly gone.
She did, and there was no heartbeat. After the procedure,
I remember thinking, I'll never have another baby again.
But over time, God healed my pain, and my youngest daughter,
Jae, was born a year and a half later.

—TERI W.

When I miscarried my baby, some friends brought us meals.
Some sent us cards. But one friend came over and sat with me
on the couch and cried with me. That was the best gift of all.

—ANN R.

FIRST-AID KIT

If You're Pregnant

★ **Care.** Get prenatal care early from a board-certified obstetrician. (You can find a list of certified OBs at www.acog.org.)

★ **Questions.** If you have any questions at all, call your OB. That's what he or she is there for!

★ **Diet.** Take prenatal vitamins and eat a balanced, healthy diet that includes protein, fruits, and vegetables.

★ **Water.** Drink lots of water to stay hydrated. Fill a 64-ounce water bottle each morning and try to drink it all by bedtime.

★ **Rest.** Try to get plenty of rest. This is the perfect time to take naps and go to bed early. Listen to your body. When you're tired, sleep!

★ **Choices.** Don't smoke or drink alcohol during your pregnancy. Be smart and be safe.

If You've Miscarried a Baby

☆ **Bleeding.** If you are cramping or bleeding, seek the advice of your doctor or midwife immediately.

☆ **Emotional healing.** Allow yourself to grieve the miscarriage. Healing won't happen overnight.

☆ **Physical healing.** Your body may still think you are pregnant, and your hormones will be racing. Get lots of extra rest and maintain a healthy diet. Now is the time to allow others to pamper you.

☆ **Husbands.** Include your husband in the grieving process. He may not grieve in the same way you do, but he will grieve in his own way. Don't shut him out.

☆ **Comfort.** Seek solace in your family and friends, especially girl-friends who have survived their own miscarriages. They have a wealth of support and encouragement to offer, and they will cry with you.

☆ **Don't worry.** Don't agonize about having another miscarriage. Know that God will cover you with His feathers and protect you under His wings (Psalm 91:4). Rest in His arms, and when you have healed, check with your doctor about when it is safe to begin trying to have another baby.

S.O.S.
(SPIRITUAL OPPORTUNITY TO SAVOR)

The wall was made of jasper, and the city of pure gold, as pure as glass. The foundations of the city walls were decorated with every kind of precious stone. The first foundation was jasper, the second sapphire, the third chalcedony, the fourth emerald, the fifth sardonyx, the sixth carnelian, the seventh chrysolite, the eighth beryl, the ninth topaz, the tenth chrysoprase, the eleventh jacinth, and the twelfth amethyst. The twelve gates were twelve pearls, each gate made of a single pearl. The great street of the city was of pure gold, like transparent glass.

REVELATION 21:18–21

 How Do I Picture Heaven?

I love reading about what heaven is like. I picture the pearl gates glowing with all kinds of colors, like the inside of a seashell, but so much brighter. I imagine the jasper foundation, the transparent streets of pure gold.

To be honest, I really didn't spend much time pondering what heaven looked like until I had my first miscarriage. That's when heaven became a real place for me, because I knew my baby was there, and I wanted to picture where he was.

Not too long after my miscarriage, my aunt Teddi fell ill and went into a coma. Mike and I decided to drive to the hospital to say good-bye to her. On that long drive north, I couldn't shake the feeling that I needed to tell her something. I knew she would soon be in heaven and would see my baby. She would get to hold him and love him.

It was selfish of me, but I almost felt panicked about getting to the hospital in time to tell Aunt Teddi to kiss my baby for me. To tell my baby I missed and loved him.

When Mike and I walked into Teddi's hospital room, all I could hear were the machines humming along in some sort of breathlike rhythm. I walked up to her bedside and laid my hands on her cheeks. I kissed her forehead and whispered my love into her ear.

I also asked her to kiss my baby for me.

She died within the hour, and my whole family misses her. But even in the midst of the sadness and loss, I feel some joy in knowing that up in heaven, Aunt Teddi is holding both my babies, playing with them and loving them.

I'm not sure we can comprehend the beauty of heaven with our earthly minds. But I am so thankful that in my glimpses of heaven, I now picture my babies with heavenly eyes.

Study Questions

1. Have you ever wondered what heaven will look like?
2. Do you think God has told us everything about heaven in the Bible? What might He be saving to show us in person?

3. Have you had a miscarriage? lost loved ones? How do you picture them in heaven?

4. Have you suffered a miscarriage? How did you find healing? How can you help others heal?

Appendix
A

Your Baby's Development

A Month-by-Month Guide

Your Newborn

- Can grasp your finger immediately if you place it in his palm.
- Will sleep a great deal from birth to three weeks of age, from twelve to twenty hours a day (though it never seems to be enough hours in a row to give Mom her needed rest).
- Does not know the difference between night and day.
- Will want to be fed every three to four hours.
- Has initial movements that are reflexes, like sucking and rooting, jerking and leg kicking.
- Can lift her head briefly while on her stomach.
- Has an amazing sense of smell and can detect your individual scent.
- Has blurry vision at first, and focuses best on objects nine to twelve inches from his face.
- Hears things in a slightly muffled way at first, which gives her an easier transition from the serene and quiet womb to the noisy world.
- Has an amplified sense of touch around his mouth.

Your One-Month-Old

- Can follow or track an object with her eyes.
- Can lift his head for a few seconds.
- Can focus on your face and recognize your voice.
- Can respond to your voice and Daddy's voice with baby noises.
- Will begin cooing to vocalize her pleasure.
- May smile in response to your own smile.
- May be able to lift his head 90 degrees when on his stomach.
- May be able to hold her head steady when upright.
- May be able to bring both hands together.

Your Two-Month-Old

- Can speak his own baby language and respond to your words with grunts and sounds.
- Enjoys it when you speak to her.
- May be able to roll over one way, usually tummy to back.
- Is comforted by daily routines.
- May laugh out loud or squeal in delight.
- Will begin to stay awake for longer periods of time.

Your Three-Month-Old

- May be able to reach for a toy.
- Shows a larger range of emotions like fascination or joy.
- Is developing a mind of his own, becoming his own person.
- Loves repetitive songs, stories, and poems.
- Loves when you read short rhyming books to her, like *Goodnight Moon.*
- Is learning a lot by experimentation.
- Will smile spontaneously.
- Is more coordinated in using his hands, and has a fascination with his fingers and toes.
- Can coo and make joyful noises when you play with her.

Your Four-Month-Old

- Is showing new interest in playing with toys.
- Might be able to roll over on his own.
- Can laugh out loud when you play with her.

- Should be able to sleep six to eight hours between feedings at night.
- Is learning how toys work by trial and error.
- Is developing memory and attention span.
- Is ready for his first solids, like baby rice cereal.

Your Five-Month-Old

- Can actually ignore distractions and focus on the task at hand.
- Is beginning to crawl and move about the house.
- Can get fussy and frustrated by her own limitations.
- May begin moving toys from one hand to the other.

Your Six-Month-Old

- May begin to use hand gestures to communicate.
- Can sit up by himself.
- Will begin mimicking your behavior, like Simon says.
- Will begin speaking in sentence-long babbles like "Da da da da."

Your Seven-Month-Old

- Is beginning to realize the cause and effect of actions and results.
- Has the pincer grasp, grasping things between her thumb and first finger.
- Loves to drop toys and watch them fall.
- May begin to grab things with one hand instead of two.
- Is beginning to develop his listening skills.

Your Eight-Month-Old

- Will stand up by pulling herself to her feet by holding on to furniture.
- Can see objects at a distance.
- Loves games like peekaboo and pat-a-cake.

Your Nine-Month-Old

- Will begin to make up his own words.
- Can solve problems like finding you when you hide behind the couch.
- May begin calling you *Mama* and Daddy *Dada*.
- Will reach out her arms when she wants to be held.

Your Ten-Month-Old

- Will imitate you when you brush your hair or teeth.
- Has learned the meaning of the word *no*.
- Will show a strong level of attachment to Mom and Dad.
- Will love banging pots and pans together to make noise.
- Will shake his head side to side to mean *no*.
- Will know where the toy is when you hide it under a blanket.

Your Eleven-Month-Old

- May begin to walk while holding on to your hands or furniture.
- May understand and use several words.
- Is developing a sense of independence and confidence in her exploration.

- Will begin saying, "Bye-bye" when you leave and waving his hand in reverse (the way he sees it when you wave).

Your One-Year-Old

- Will begin to want to do things by herself.
- May begin walking independently and fall down a lot.
- May respond to as many as fifty words.
- Walks like a duck with his feet spread far apart, leaning side to side.
- Can respond to simple questions like "Where's your nose?" by pointing to her nose.
- Will give you an open-mouthed, sloppy kiss when you ask him for a kiss.

Your Compass

Resources for Surviving the First Year

Breast-Feeding

Breast-feeding online resources—http://breastfeeding.com
International Lactation Consultant Association—www.ilca.org
La Leche League: Breast-feeding support group
   www.lalecheleague.org

Bottle-Feeding

The Enfamil Web site—www.Enfamil.com
What About Babies: Your Online Guide to Everything Babies—
   www.whataboutbabies.com

Dads

A Father's Legacy by Gary Smalley, John Trent, Greg Vaughn, Fred
   Holmes (Focus on the Family)
National Fatherhood Initiative—www.fatherhood.org

Dinnertime

Books:

*The Great American Supper Swap: Solving the Busy Woman's Family
   Dinnertime Dilemma!* by Trish Berg—www.trishberg.com
Once-a-Month Cooking by Mary Beth Lagerborg and Mimi Wilson
Food That Says Welcome: Simple Recipes to Spark the Spirit of Hospitality
   by Barbara Smith
*Cooking Among Friends: Meal Planning and Preparation Delightfully
   Simplified* by Mary Tennant and Becki Visser

Recipe Web sites:

Trish's Recipe of the Week—www.trishberg.com

www.allrecipes.com (My favorite for FAST printable recipes!)

www.bestsimplerecipes.com

www.bettycrocker.com

www.pillsbury.com

Due Dates

March of Dimes Due Date Calculator—
www.marchofdimes.com/pnhec/1808_1892.asp

Epidurals

American Medical Association—www.ama-assn.org

Information on epidurals—www.the-health-pages.com/topics/
education/epidural.html

Family Life

*Building the Christian Family You Never Had: A Practical Guide for
Pioneer Parents* by Mary DeMuth (Colorado Springs, CO:
WaterBrook Press, 2006)—www.marydemuth.com

The Strong Family: Growing Wise in Family Life by Charles R. Swindoll
(Grand Rapids, MI: Zondervan, 1994)

www.familylife.com

Financial Resources

Crown Financial Ministries—www.crown.org

A Girl and Her Money by Sharon Durling—http://sharondurling.com

A Mom's Guide to Family Finances by Ellie Kay (Grand Rapids, MI: Revell, 2006)—www.elliekay.com

Debt-Proof Your Marriage: How to Achieve Financial Harmony by Mary Hunt (Grand Rapids, MI: Revell, 2004)—www.cheapskatemonthly.com

Dollars & Sense: A Mom's Guide to Money Matters by Cynthia Sumner (Grand Rapids, MI: Revell, 2005)—www.cynthiasumner.com

Fun

Award-winning books by Jackie Silberg: *125 Brain Games for Babies,* 1999; *Games to Play with Babies,* 3rd ed., 2001; *Games to Play with Toddlers,* rev., 2002; *Games to Play with Two Year Olds,* rev., 2002; *More Games to Play with Toddlers,* 1996; all from Gryphon House (Beltsville, MD)—www.ghbooks.com

Health Issues for Mom

A Woman's Guide to Good Health (Grand Rapids, MI: Revell, 2006); and *Mom's Health Matters* (Grand Rapids, MI: Zondervan, 2003); both books by Carrie Carter, MD—www.carteronhealth.com

Marriage

The Five Love Languages: How to Express Heartfelt Commitment to Your Mate by Gary Chapman, reissue (Chicago: Northfield, 1995)

Love for a Lifetime: Building a Marriage That Will Go the Distance by Dr. James Dobson (Sisters, OR: Multnomah, 1994)—www.family.org

Love Talk: Speak Each Other's Language Like You Never Have Before by Drs. Les and Leslie Parrott (Grand Rapids, MI: Zondervan, 2004)—www.realrelationships.com

When Husband and Wife Become Mom and Dad by Elisa Morgan and
   Carol Kuykendall, MOPS International (Grand Rapids, MI: Zondervan, 2000)—www.mops.org

Marriage Conferences

A Weekend to Remember—www.familylife.com
Peacemaker Marriage—www.familylife.com
Improving Communication—www.familylife.com

Miscarriage

MEND: Mommies Enduring Neonatal Death: Christian, nonprofit
   organization that reaches out to families who have suffered the loss of
   a baby through miscarriage, stillbirth, or early infant death—
   http://home.mend.org
March of Dimes: Facts and Information About Miscarriages—
   www.marchofdimes.com
Christian Miscarriage Support Group—
   www.missionaryresources.com/miscarriage.html
Fertility Plus: Christian Links for Women Suffering Miscarriages—
   www.fertilityplus.org/faq/miscarriage/resources.html

Motherhood

Simplifying Motherhood Web site—www.trishberg.com
*Ordinary Mom, Extraordinary God: Encouragement to Refresh Your
   Soul* by Mary DeMuth (Eugene, OR: Harvest House, 2005)—
   www.marydemuth.com

Parenting Power in the Early Years: Raising Your Child with Confidence—
  Birth to Age Five by Brenda Nixon (Enumclaw, WA: Winepress,
  2001)—www.brendanixon.com

She's Gonna Blow!: Real Help for Moms Dealing with Anger (2005) and
  Motherhood: The Guilt That Keeps on Giving (2006), both by Julie
  Ann Barnhill (Eugene, OR: Harvest House)—ww.juliebarnhill.com

Time Out for Mom…Ahhh Moments by Cynthia Sumner and Mary
  Beth Lagerborg (Grand Rapids, MI: Zondervan, 2000)—
  www.cynthiasumner.com

Women's Conferences

Hearts at Home—www.hearts-at-home.org

Women of Faith—www.womenoffaith.com

Mothers of Preschoolers (MOPS) International—www.mops.org

Obstetricians

American College of Obstetricians and Gynecologists—www.acog.org

Pediatricians

Find the right pediatrician for your child—www.aap.org/referral

Postpartum Depression

Family Doctor Online—http://familydoctor.org/379.xml

Postpartum Support International Hotline—www.postpartum.net, or
  call 1-800-944-4PPD

Mayo Clinic—www.mayoclinic.com

Reflux (GERD)

American Academy of Family Physicians—www.familydoctor.org

RSV

The RSV Information Center (Respiratory Syncytial Virus)—
www.rsvinfo.com/

SIDS

American SIDS Institute—www.sids.org
The SIDS & Infant Death Survival Guide—http://sidssurvivalguide.org

Sleep

Getting Your Baby to Sleep Through the Night—
www.askdrsears.com/html/7/T070300.asp

Notes

Introduction

1. Inspired by Tim Bete, *In the Beginning, There Were No Diapers: Laughing and Learning in the First Years of Fatherhood* (Notre Dame, IN: Sorin Books, 2005), 23–25.

Chapter 1

1. David J. Demko, "Mean Age Moms Ladies in Waiting," *Age Venture News Service,* December 12, 2002, www.demko.com/m021212.htm (accessed June 2006).

2. "High-Risk Newborn: Postmaturity," University of Virginia Health Systems, www.healthsystem.virginia.edu/uvahealth/peds_hrnewborn/postmtur.cfm (accessed May 2006).

3. Leah Albers, "How Long Is Normal Labor?" Summary of a presentation by Leah Albers, CNM, DrPH, at the 46th ACNM Annual Meeting, School of Medicine at the University of New Mexico, June 8, 2006, www.midwife info.com/content/view/68/45/ (accessed June 2007).

4. William Camann and Kathryn Alexander, *Easy Labor* (New York: Ballantine/Random House, 2006), excerpted by permission of Ballantine Books, a division of Random House, Inc., www.randomhouse.com/rhpg/catalog/display.pperl?isbn=9780345476630&view=excerpt (accessed May 2006).

5. A. B. Goldberg, A. Cohen, E. Lieberman, "Nulliparas' Preferences for Epidural Analgesia: Their Effects on Actual Use in Labor," www.pubmed.gov, www.ncbi.nlm.nih.gov/entrez/query.fcgi?cmd=Retrieve&db=PubMed&list_uids=10655812&dopt=Abstract (accessed May 2006).

6. "Pain Relief for Childbirth," UC Davis Health System, Sacramento, CA, www.ucdmc.ucdavis.edu/pulse/scripts/00_01/pain_relief_for_childbirth%20.pdf (accessed May 2006).

7. "Eating for Two: Weight Influences on Pregnancy," American Pregnancy Association, www.americanpregnancy.org/pregnancyhealth/eatingfortwo.html (accessed June 2006).

Chapter 2

1. "Singletons and Multiples Overview," March of Dimes, peristats, www.marchofdimes.com/peristats/tlanding.aspx?reg=99&lev=0&top=7 &slev=1&dv=qf (accessed July 2007).

2. "Sleep Basics: Printout Guide," Parents.com, © Meredith Corp., www.parents.com/parents/story.jhtml?storyid=/templatedata/parents/story/ data/1113.xml (accessed June 2006).

3. "Let Sleep Work for You," National Sleep Foundation, www.sleepfoundation.org/site/c.huIXKjM0IxF/b.2421185/k.7198/ Let_Sleep_Work_for_You.htm (accessed July 2007).

4. Laurie LaRusso, MS ELS, "Breast-feeding may reduce the risk of breast cancer," St. David's HealthCare, http://healthlibrary.epnet.com/getcontent.aspx? siteid=1a0b79c6-1489-11d4-81d4-00508b1249d5&docid=/journalnotes/ breastfeedcx (accessed June 2006).

5. "Breastfeeding: the Numbers," www.kellymom.com/writings/ bf-numbers.html#usa (accessed 27 June 2006).

6. "Bottle-Feeding Your Baby," www.drugs.com/cg/bottle_feeding_ your_baby.html (accessed June 2006).

7. LaRusso, "Breast-feeding may reduce the risk of breast cancer."

Chapter 3

1. Inspired by "Brilliant Baby and Toddler Tips," *Parents,* July 2006, 127–130.

2. Stephen F. Duncan, Ph.D., "The Importance of Fathers," Montana State University, www.montana.edu/wwwpb/pubs/mt2000-08.html (accessed June 2006).

3. Kemba J. Dunham, "Stay-at-Home Dads Face a Career-Limiting Stigma," *Wall Street Journal Online,* www.careerjournal.com/myc/workfamily/ 20030902-dunham.html (accessed June 2006).

4. "Selecting and Using the Most Appropriate Car Safety Seats for Growing Children: Guidelines for Counseling Parents," *Pediatrics,* vol. 109, no. 3, March 2002, 550–53, http://aappolicy.aappublications.org/cgi/content/ full/pediatrics;109/3/550 (accessed May 2007).

Chapter 4

1. Shaunti Feldhahn, *For Women Only* (Sisters, OR: Multnomah, 2004), 14.

2. Feldhahn, *For Women Only*, 15.

3. "Health Bites," *Psychology Today*, May/June 2005, www.psychologytoday.com/articles/pto-20050506-000003.html (accessed June 2006).

4. Lorilee Craker, *We Should Do This More Often: A Parents' Guide to Romance, Passion, and Other Prechild Activities You Vaguely Recall* (Colorado Springs, CO: WaterBrook Press, 2005), 3.

5. Hara Estroff Marano, "A New Focus on Family Values," *Psychology Today*, Nov/Dec 1997, www.psychologytoday.com/articles/pto-19971101-000028.html (accessed June 2006).

6. Inspired by "Keys to a Successful Marriage," Garden of Praise Web site, www.gardenofpraise.com/keys.htm (accessed 20 June 2006).

Chapter 5

1. Gary Chapman and Ross Campbell, *The Five Love Languages of Children* (Chicago: Northfield, 1997), 30.

2. Colin Allen, "Shy for Life," *Psychology Today*, June 23, 2003, www.psychologytoday.com/articles/index.php?term=pto-20030623000001.xml&print=1 (accessed June 2006).

3. Joanna Lipari, "Raising Baby: What You Need to Know," *Psychology Today*, July/Aug 2000, http://www.psychologytoday.com/articles/pto-20000701000033.html (accessed June 2006).

4. "The Evolution of Mom," *Mothers' Day World*, www.mothersdayworld.com/mothers-day-humor/evolution-of-mother.html (accessed June 2006).

Chapter 6

1. "Statistics," Organizing Resources, www.organizingresources.com/1stats.htm (accessed May 2006).

2. FlyLady, www.flylady.com (accessed June 2006).

Chapter 7

1. Heide Lang, "The Trouble with Day Care," *Psychology Today,* May/June 2005, www.psychologytoday.com/articles/pto-20050504-000004.htmlIBID (accessed on June 2006).

2. Lesley Stahl, "Staying at Home," *60 Minutes,* October 10, 2004, CBSNews.com, excerpt, www.cbsnews.com/stories/2004/10/08/60minutes/main648240.shtml (accessed July 2007).

3. "Returning to the Workplace," Salary.com, www.salary.com/aboutus/layoutscripts/abtl_default.asp?tab=abt&cat=cat012&ser=ser041&part=Par481 (accessed July 2007).

4. "Not for the Money," *Psychology Today,* May 1992, www.psychologytoday.com/articles/pto-19920501-000018.html (accessed June 2006).

5. Lang, "The Trouble with Day Care."

6. Sloan Work and Family Research Network, Boston College, "Statistics: Part-Time Work and Women," http://wfnetwork.bc.edu/statistics_template.php?id=1646&topic=10&area=academics (accessed June 2006).

7. Sloan, "Statistics: Part-Time Work: What Are People Doing Before Working Part-Time?" http://wfnetwork.bc.edu/statistics_template.php?id=1648&topic=10&area=academics (accessed June 2006).

8. Sloan, "Statistics."

Chapter 8

1. Sharon Jayson, "Marriage's Relative Discord," *USA Today,* www.usatoday.com/life/lifestyle/2005-05-16-mother-in-law-relationships_x.htm (accessed June 2006).

2. Kenneth W. Howard, "Thorn: In-Laws," The Bible Network, www.siscom.net/•direct/marriage_inlaws (accessed June 2006).

3. Abigail Trafford, "More Meat in the Middle," *The Washington Post,* May 16, 2006, www.washingtonpost.com/wp-dyn/content/article/2006/05/15/AR2006051501145.html (accessed June 2006).

4. Howard, "Thorn: In-Laws."

5. Terri Apter, "Mothers-in-law and Daughters-in-law: Friendship at an Impasse," University of Cambridge, www.motherinlawstories.com/terri_apter_research_paper.htm (accessed June 2006).

Chapter 9

1. Robert Provine, "The Science of Laughter," *Psychology Today,* Nov/Dec 2000, www.psychologytoday.com/articles/pto-20001101-000036.html (accessed June 2006).

2. Provine, "Science of Laughter."

3. University of Maryland Medical Center, "Laughter Is Good for Your Heart, According to a New University of Maryland Medical Center Study," news release, November 15, 2000, www.umm.edu/news/releases/laughter.html (accessed June 2006).

4. Rod A. Martin, "Do Children Laugh Much More Often Than Adults Do?" Association for Applied and Therapeutic Humor, June 14, 2006, http://aath.org/articles/art_martin.html (accessed June 2006).

5. Martin, "Do Children Laugh?"

6. Valerie Frankel, "Laugh It Up!" *Parenting,* October 2003, www.parenting.com/parenting/article/0,19840,648261,00.html (accessed June 2006).

Chapter 10

1. Jennifer Tzeses, "The Safety Mistakes Even Good Moms Make," *Parenting,* April 2004, www.parenting.com/parenting/child/article/0,19840,648459,00.html (accessed June 2006).

Chapter 11

1. "Re: Palooza." The Phrase Finder Web site, www.phrases.org.uk/bulletin_board/14/messages/210.html (accessed June 2006).

2. "Your Play Personality," The Institute for Play, www.instituteforplay.com/4your_play_personality.htm (accessed June 2006).

3. "New Research on Brain Development Is Important for Parents," Child Care Aware—*The Daily Parent,* vol. 1, www.childcareaware.org/en/dailyparent/volume.php?id=1 (accessed June 2006).

4. "Helping Your Child Make Connections—Making the Most of the Brain Gain," Child Care Aware—*The Daily Parent,* vol. 36, www.childcareaware.org/en/dailyparent/volume.php?id=40 (accessed June 2006).

5. "Show Them the Moves—Get Your Children Active for Life," Child Care Aware—*The Daily Parent,* vol. 38, www.childcareaware.org/en/dailyparent/volume.php?id=38 (accessed June 2006).

Chapter 12

1. "Prayer and Healing," Duke University News and Communications, November 30, 2001, www.dukenews.duke.edu/2001/11/mm_prayerand.html (accessed June 2007).

2. David N. Elkins, "Spirituality," *Psychology Today,* Sept/Oct 1999, www.psychologytoday.com/articles/pto-19990901-000036.html (accessed June 2006).

3. Elkins, "Spirituality."

4. Erik Ness, "Does Prayer Heal?" *New York Daily News,* November 15, 2005, www.columbia.edu/cu/news/clips/2005/11/16/doesprayerDAILYNEWS.pdf (accessed June 2006).

Chapter 13

1. "Lose the Baby Weight—for Good!" *Babytalk,* August 2005, www.parenting.com/parenting/mom/article/0,19840,1084734,00.html (accessed June 2006).

2. Inspired by Pamela Redmond Satran, "10 Things to Do With Your Pre-Pregnancy Jeans," *Babytalk,* October 2003, www.parenting.com/parenting/article/0,19840,648285,00.html (accessed July 2007).

3. Fast Stats A to Z: Heart Disease, National Center for Health Statistics, www.cdc.gov/nchs/fastats/heart.htm (accessed June 2007).

4. Fast Stats A to Z: Exercise/Physical Activity, Summary Health Statistics for U.S. Adults: National Health Interview Survey, 2005, table 29, National Center for Health Statistics, www.cdc.gov/nchs/fastats/exercise.htm (accessed June 2006).

5. David Garner, "Survey Says: Body Image Poll Results," *Psychology Today,* February 1997, www.psychologytoday.com (accessed June 2006).

6. Garner, "Body Image."

Chapter 14

1. "Health Bites," *Psychology Today,* May/June 2005, www.psychologytoday.com/articles/pto-20050506-000003.html (accessed June 2006).

2. Sharon Jayson, Sidebar: "Sexes Treat Friendships Differently," USA TODAY, December 19, 2005, www.usatoday.com/news/nation/2005-12-19-friendships-cover_x.htm (accessed June 2006).

3. Gale Berkowitz, "UCLA Study on Friendship Among Women: An alternative to fight or flight," 2002, www.anapsid.org/cnd/gender/tendfend.html (accessed June 2006).

4. Berkowitz, "UCLA Study."

5. Berkowitz, "UCLA Study."

6. MOPS International Web site, www.mops.org/page.php?pageid=70&srctype=menu (accessed June 2006).

7. Based on David G. Myers, "Pursuing Happiness," *Psychology Today,* July/Aug 1993, excerpted from David G. Myers, *The Pursuit of Happiness* (New York: Avon, 1993), www.psychologytoday.com/articles/pto-19930701-000026.html (accessed June 2006).

Afterword

1. Author unknown, "The Cost of Raising a Child," Surf-in-the-Spirit, www.surfinthespirit.com/finances/child.html (accessed June 2006).

2. "The Cost of Raising a Child."

Discovering the Footprints of Heaven

1. Dr. Eric Daiter, "Miscarriages Tutorial," InfertilityTutorials.com, The New Jersey Center for Fertility and Reproductive Medicine, www.thenewjerseymiscarriagecenter.com/incidence_rate.php (accessed August 2007).

2. "About D&C for Miscarriage," American College of Surgeons, www.facs.org, www.facs.org/public_info/operation/dncmiss.pdf (accessed May 2007).

3. Linda DeYmaz, *Mommy, Please Don't Cry* (Sisters, OR: Multnomah, 1996), 1–4, 23–26.